WHEN
GOD
DIED

WHEN
GOD
DIED

HERBERT
LOCKYER

W
WHITAKER
HOUSE

Unless otherwise indicated, all Scripture quotations are taken from the King James Version of the Holy Bible. Scripture quotations marked (WEY) are taken from *The New Testament in Modern Speech: An Idiomatic Translation into Everyday English from the Text of "The Resultant Greek Testament"* by R. F. (Richard Francis) Weymouth.

Boldface type in the Scripture quotations indicates the author's emphasis.

WHEN GOD DIED:
A Series of Meditations for Lent

ISBN: 978-1-62911-296-1
eBook ISBN: 978-1-62911-297-8
Printed in the United States of America
© 2015 by Ardis A. Lockyer

Whitaker House
1030 Hunt Valley Circle
New Kensington, PA 15068
www.whitakerhouse.com

Library of Congress Cataloging-in-Publication Data

Lockyer, Herbert.
  When God died : a series of meditations for Lent / by Herbert Lockyer.
    pages cm
  Includes bibliographical references.
    ISBN 978-1-62911-296-1 (trade pbk. : alk. paper) — ISBN 978-1-62911-297-8
  (ebook) 1. Jesus Christ—Crucifixion—Meditations. I. Title.
  BT450.L63 2015
  242'.34—dc23
                                    2014045499

1 2 3 4 5 6 7 8 9 10 11 ᰃᰃ 22 21 20 19 18 17 16 15

CONTENTS

PREFACE

It is more than likely that some readers of this volume will take exception to its title. How could God, the deathless One, die? To declare that, at the cross, God was actually slain is to impugn the eternal unity of the Godhead.

Well, is it more difficult to believe that the second Person of the Trinity died at Calvary than it is to hold that He was made man at His birth? Could God have a birth? Could He—a Spirit—become a man? We readily accept the fact although we cannot explain the mystery of it, that God, the Son, had a birth; that He not only assumed a human form, as in some of His theophanic appearances, but that He was actually made man. He was born of a woman! As God, He was manifest in the flesh! The Ancient of Days had a birthday! The everlasting Father became a *"babe wrapped in swaddling clothes"* (Luke 2:12).

Believing, then, in the wonder of the incarnation, surely it is not harder to accept the sublime revelation that He who was God's equal and had full deity died upon the tree. Here are a few passages to ponder:

> *God will provide **himself** the lamb for a burnt offering.*
> (Genesis 22:8)

> *Behold the Lamb of God, which taketh away the sin of the world.*
> (John 1:29)

> *...the church of God, which he [God] hath purchased with his own blood.* (Acts 20:28)

What is this but the death of Deity! God spilling His blood in order to acquire the church! "*God was in Christ, reconciling the world unto himself*" (2 Corinthians 5:19). God in Christ? Yes, not only representatively but intrinsically. Christ Himself was God. "*I and the Father are one*" (John 10:30).

There are some who vainly try to separate our Lord's two natures, claiming that it was Jesus, the human One, who died. God within His body was dismissed before His decease. Such, however, is false reasoning, for the fusion of deity and humanity in the Virgin's womb was of an indissoluble nature.

Did Christ die as God, or did He die as man? The answer to such a question is that He died as neither. What gives efficacy to the cross is the fact that Christ died as the God-man. Thus a more correct caption for the following "Passion" messages might be "When the God-man Died."

How slow we are to learn that the incarnation of our Lord brought about a distinct change in the composition of the Trinity. Hitherto, the Father, Son, and Holy Spirit were coequal in that each was a spirit. None of the Persons of the Godhead possessed permanent corporeality. Since the entrance of Christ into our humanity, however, the Trinity has been composed of two Members who retained their eternal spirit form and one Member who surrendered His spirit form for corporeality.

Christ is no longer a spirit. Beholding Christ after His resurrection, His frightened disciples took Him to be a spirit, but with that assuring voice of His, Jesus said, "*Handle me, and see;...for a spirit hath not flesh and bones, as ye see me have*" (Luke 24:39). Flesh and bones are part of the Trinity now. O the wonder of it! There is a body in the Godhead, seeing that the Godhead is in a body. (See Colossians 2:9.)

Think for a minute of the marvelous work of the Holy Spirit within Mary. It was he who was commissioned to bring about the merger of deity and humanity. Laying hold of God, the Son, the Spirit wove Him into the texture of Mary's flesh, thereby becoming the love knot between our Lord's two natures. Thus Christ appeared among men not as God exclusively or as Man exclusively but as the God-man, the Holy Spirit's superb creation. And in this unique form, He lived among men and ultimately died upon the cross. The blood He shed, therefore, has abiding efficacy, seeing that it was the blood of an extraordinary nature, namely, the blood of God and Man combined. If He died simply as a man, then the blood He shed has no more efficacy than the blood that streamed from the riven veins of the two thieves who were His companions in death that dark day.

And, let it never be forgotten that the perpetual wonder of heaven since the Ascension has been some of humanity's dust, glorified, seated upon the throne. Within the Godhead is now a Great High Priest, touched with the feelings of our infirmities, seeing that He took back to His position in the Trinity the human body the Holy Spirit gave Him at His birth. What else can we do but adore the Father, Son, and Holy Spirit for Their bountiful provision on our behalf!

> Alas! and did my Savior bleed,
> And did my Sovereign die!
> Would he devote that sacred head
> For sinners such as I?

***

> Well might the sun in darkness hide,
> And shut its glories in,
> When God, the mighty maker, died
> For his own creature's sin.[1]

—*Herbert Lockyer*

---

1. Isaac Watts, "Alas, and Did My Savior Bleed," 1707.

1

THE CHRIST OF THE CROSS

"Behold the man!"
—John 19:5

Each of the four Gospels is necessary to give us a perfect portrait of Him who exceeds all description. Each or the Gospels gives us a different view of the Lord Jesus Christ. Matthew, for example, cries, "Behold the King!" Mark, "Behold the Servant!" Luke, "Behold the Man!" John, "Behold the God!"

The chapter, however, from which our basic verse is taken combines so many sublime presentations of Christ. In a masterful way, John depicts the many-sided person of the Lord he dearly loved. His profiles of Christ are introduced by the exclamation "Behold." (See, for example, John 19:4–5, 14, 26–27.) And this simple yet significant term calls attention to something striking, unique, and wonderful. Wherever it occurs, there follows an arrestive thought, fact, or message. (See Revelation 3:20.)

Quite recently, I found it interesting to trace the use of this exclamation in John's gospel. Take, for instance, the first and last appearances, and note their connection. *"Behold the Lamb of God"* (John 1:29) and *"Behold my hands"* (John 20:27). The first was uttered before the cross, the latter after the cross. The first reveals the One who was ready and who was soon to be offered; the latter shows us the slain, victorious Lamb. Thomas saw the nail prints John the Baptist preached of but never witnessed.

HIS HOLINESS

Thrice over John affirms the sinlessness of Jesus. *"Behold…*[there is] *no fault in Him"* (John 19:4). What a coveted reputation to have! Without fault or flaw. Dr. Weymouth translates it, *"No crime in him"* (John 19:4 wey). There was no proof, whatever, of treason against Caesar. No fault! No crime! What a confession for a heathen monarch to make! It is possible for us to be blameless but not faultless. Jesus, however, was both blameless and faultless. In all His dealings with God and man, there was absolute rectitude. So beholding Him as the sinless One, we believe Him. There He stood in Pilate's hall, God's perfect Man, man's perfect God. (See Hebrews 7:26.)

HIS HUMANITY

"Ecce homo!" "Behold the man!" (John 19:5) Language fails to describe the utter humiliation of our blessed Lord as He trudged the bloodred way leading to His cross. Let us try to depict the scene before us. There stands the faultless One—pale, bleeding, exhausted, and helpless. Pilate, as a last resort, appealed to the crowd for pity. Will no one in the throng lift up his voice in mercy and plead to save this sorry spectacle of suffering from death? No, the bound and bleeding form of Jesus could not elicit any sympathy. Pilate's appeal fell on deaf ears. In fact, his voice was hardly heard amid the insistent cries for the blood of the innocent Man standing before him.

But is there not a deeper truth in the ruler's exclamation, *"Behold the man!"*? Truly, He became the Man Christ Jesus. He wrapped Himself with the garment of our humanity to win and save mankind. And as a Man, sorrows, weariness, pain, tears, hunger, and other physical needs were His. We behold Him as the Man tempted in all points like as we are. As the Man, He understands all about our human needs; and as God, He can meet them all.

HIS HONOR

Seeing that his appeal for pity fails, Pilate now poured scorn upon Christ's rejecters. He goaded them with the cynical taunt *"Behold your*

King!" (John 19:14). There Jesus rose to a position where all the Jews could see Him. What a pitiable sight He presented on that dark day! Hands bound, thorn crowned, clad in an old military cloak, and yet Pilate cried, *"Your King!"* It may be that he heard of Christ's triumphal entry into Jerusalem but a few days before, when the populace acclaimed Him as Messiah. Or possibly he thought of our Lord's own claim, *"Thou sayest that I am a king. To this end was I born"* (John 18:37).

In the original, the *"your"* is emphatic. The people, however, had reached the depth of degradation in their abandonment of messianic hopes, hence their rejection of Christ and their desire for His death.

Let us behold this King standing there clad in the mock insignia of royalty. What a travesty of a coronation for One who was a king indeed!

If He is a King, then He must have a throne; and He had it in the stump over which He was placed as His back was lashed.

If He is a King, then He must have a crown; and He had it in the thorn-circlet adorning His brow.

If He is a King, then He must have a robe; and He had it in some gaudy military jacket discarded by a soldier.

If He is a King, then He must have a scepter; and He had it in the reed, the symbol of weakness, thrust into His hand.

If He is a King, then He must have homage; and He had it in the mock worship of those who cried, *"Hail, King of the Jews!"* (Matthew 27:29; Mark 15:18; John 19:3).

His anguish has passed, however, and we see Jesus crowned with honor and glory as the result of His cross. (See Hebrews 2:9.) May we never be guilty of crucifying the King, or of giving Him a mock coronation! This we do when we honor Him with our lips but have hearts that are far from Him. Let us endeavor to be among the true subjects who, loving Him, bring forth the royal diadem and crown Him Lord of all.

HIS HEROISM

"Behold thy son!" (See John 19:26.) This dying word of Christ's has a twofold significance. First of all, it can apply to John, the beloved

disciple. Seeing his companion whom He dearly loved, Jesus said to Mary, His mother, *"Behold thy son!"* (John 19:26). As if to say, "I am of no further use to you, but here is John, My favorite disciple. He will fill My place and do duty as a son." Take note that our Lord did not employ the term *mother*, lest He identify her with Himself and thereby expose her to danger and to the ridicule of the crowd. But with characteristic tenderness, He committed Mary to the care of one He loved beyond others, because, beyond others, John had received His love. Thus, in some measure, John stepped into the vacant place left by his Friend.

The exclamation before us can also be applied to Jesus Himself. Such a statement—*"Behold thy son!"*—can indicate not only our Lord's humanity but the fact that He was Mary's own Son, and that, therefore, they were very dear to each other. No matter what others may have thought of Christ as He endured the agonies of the cross, to Mary, He was her Son. And who knows, perhaps our Lord drew attention to Himself in this way hoping that the heroic way in which He was dying, the innocent for the guilty, would inspire His mother to bravely watch by Him, as she did to the bitter end.

It may be fitting to observe that twice over Jesus called His mother "Woman" (John 2:4; John 19:26). In His day, there was nothing disrespectful about the term, for it was used to address women of highest rank, as we use the term *lady* today.

"Woman, what have I to do with thee?" (John 2:4). Such a question was not uttered in the spirit of faultfinding, as if Christ were rebuking His mother for her interference. Another version translates the passage, *"Leave the matter in my hands"* (John 2:4 WEY).

"Woman, behold thy son!" (John 19:26). It would seem as if there was a contradiction between these two statements. In the first occurrence, Jesus disclaims any connection with His mother; in the second, He affirms it. Yet there is no contradiction between the two. Ties hitherto were bound to give way to higher obligations. Now His movements must be determined by the counsels of God, and He became subject to such, even as He had been subject to His mother. But when, with the cross, the will of God had been realized, Christ brings Mary back

again to the human side and reveals how heroically He could die both as God's Son and her Son. And so, Mary stood by the cross to pay her last respects to her illustrious Child, and then help to bury the One she had been privileged to bear.

HIS HUMANENESS

Addressing John the beloved, Jesus said, *"Behold thy mother!"* (John 19:27). What tender consideration is emphasized here! How thoughtful Jesus is! He was not so wrapped up in His own suffering as to forget the future of her who had shielded Him for thirty happy years. Thus, amid the shame and sorrow of His bitter death, His humaneness and His thoughtfulness for others relieve the utter brutality expressed in other directions. And do we not learn from our Lord's example the necessary lesson of consideration? When the dark shadows fall, we must not allow them to shut out all thought of others.

But this beautiful word that fell from the parched lips of Jesus also instructed John to act the part of son to Mary after His death. Thus, Jesus exhorts him to take His place. And here is a double committal, for John is to *find* as well as to *give* sympathy. Sympathy in their common loss was to be a source of love to each other.

Jesus knew what a heartbroken, lonely woman His mother would be after He was gone, for had He not experienced the pang of parting as He left the ivory palaces for a world of sin and woe? He knew that Simeon's word about a sword piercing Mary's heart was about to be fulfilled, as with tearful eyes, she lovingly beheld her Son. But as He gazed on her, He showed the utmost consideration by providing her with a future home. He revealed His tender care by consigning her to the tender protection of His bosom friend, John.

He had no silver or gold or possessions to leave His mother, yet He did the next best. Plundered of all, the Lord had nothing to bequeath, but what precious gifts He bestowed—pardon for His murderers, paradise for His companion in suffering, a loving home with His beloved friend for His mother, Mary.

If we are called upon to shelter, succor, and care for another, affording him the comfort of a home whether he has any claim on us or not, then may we know that by our provision, we are but following the steps of Him who desired a home for the sorrowing mother who had birthed Him.

No mention of Joseph, Mary's husband, may indicate that he had died. In fact, legend has it that he passed away when Jesus was but a lad and that the burden of home and business fell upon His shoulders. If Joseph had been alive at Christ's death, there would have been no need for Christ to commit Mary to the care of another.

It is affirmed by some scholars that the *"brethren"* mentioned in John 2:12 were stepbrothers, suggesting that after Joseph's decease, Mary remarried, and the children from this marriage became the opponents of Christ's claim. Sometimes there are ill-feelings and lack of true love and sympathy among stepsiblings from homes of remarriage. But there are many happy exceptions.

Apart from these conjectures, however, the fact remains that our Lord was ever thoughtful of His mother, and that in committing her to John, He knew that she would be content to live with him because of their mutual love for Jesus. And, because spiritual friends are ever the best ones to have, let us cultivate the fellowship of such. By helping and praying for one another, we thereby enable each other to bear the unresponsive relationships of life. We live in a cold, loveless world; and often, there is not humaneness on the part of children toward their parents as Jesus manifested when He provided a comfortable abode for His mother, who was in His thoughts as He died.

What necessary lessons affecting the ordinary relationships of life we can learn from the Christ of the cross! He is ever our Exemplar, and we are wise indeed if we are willing to plant our feet in His footprints and follow such wherever they may lead.

2

THE CROWN OF THORNS

"Then came Jesus forth, wearing the crown of thorns."
—John 19:5

The mock crowning of the Savior was only one of the many indignities He willingly endured throughout His final days of suffering. Yet how full of spiritual import for our reverent, adoring hearts is the sight of the thorn-crowned Victim of Calvary.

That ugly crown platted by the soldiers was not only a mock one but a circlet of torture, piercing deep into Christ's lovely brow. Already He had experienced severe scourging; now His hands were bound, which meant that they could not apply a softening touch to the place of pain. His fingers, easing many an aching heart, were not able to lift the garland of spikes to thereby relieve the smart, the torture of His own bleeding brow.

And since the Master's willingness to wear that crown of sharp, poisonous thorns was the fact that John so graphically depicts, let us endeavor to understand how such a coronation adds to His majesty.

HIS CONDESCENSION

To wear such a crown, Christ had to lay aside His crown of past glory. *Rich, yet for [our] sake[s] he became poor"* (2 Corinthians 8:9). And it is only when we compare the honor He received from the retinue of heaven with the shame and rejection of earth that we realize something of what was involved in that voluntary surrender of His.

Think of it! He left a world of glory for one of meanness—one of bliss for one of misery—one of purity for one of crime—one of life for one of death. He who was the eternal King was treated as a criminal, as the offscouring of the earth. He who created worlds by the word of His power is sold for the price of a common slave. He who came as the blessed Emancipator of souls was bound as a felon and led out to die. He who justly possessed the royalties of heaven suffered the ignominies of earth. He who had borne and will yet bear the crown of universal dominion was diademed with a ring of thorns. He who is and ever will be the fountain of bliss died in the anguish of thirst. Truly such condescension enables us to sing with Stephen the Sabaite,

> Is there diadem, as monarch,
> That His brow adorns?
> "Yea, a crown in very surety,
> But of thorns!

HIS EXALTATION

Christ's crown of mockery, however, has added greater glory to His eternal crown of honor.

> The head that once was crowned with thorns
> Is crowned with glory now.[2]

It is not the weight of gold composing a crown or the costly jewels bedecking it that determine its value and worth, but the character of the one whose brow it adorns. Judged thus, what dignity is associated with the crown of thorns worn by the Purest of the pure. Had these coarse soldiers only known it, every thorn was but a jewel inwrought with that of Christ's divine majesty. The cruel scorn of man He has transformed into the emblem of divine regal power. Humbled, He has been highly exalted. Treated as a felon, He yet died a King, withal in disguise. The crown He presently wears is more beauteous because of the chaplet of thorns. Here is a quote from Charles Spurgeon's *Morning and Evening*:

---

2. Thomas Kelly, "The Head That Once Was Crowned," 1820.

An instructive writer has made a sad list of the honors that the blinded people of Israel awarded to their long-expected King. First, they gave Him a procession of honor, in which Roman legionaries, Jewish priests, men, and women took part, He Himself bearing His cross. This is the triumph that the world awards to Him who comes to overthrow man's direst foes. Derisive shouts are His only acclamations and cruel taunts His only tributes of praise. Next, they presented Him with the wine of honor. Instead of a golden cup of generous wine, they offered Him the criminal's stupefying death-draught, which He refused because He would preserve an uninjured taste wherewith to taste of death. Afterward, when He cried, *"I thirst"* (John 19:28), they gave Him vinegar mixed with gall, thrust to His mouth on a sponge. Oh, wretched, detestable inhospitality to the King's Son. Third, He was provided with a guard of honor, who showed their esteem of Him by gambling over His garments, which they had seized as their booty. Such was the bodyguard of the adored of heaven—a quartet of brutal gamblers. Then a throne of honor was found for Him on the bloody tree; no easier place of rest would rebellious men yield to their faithful Lord. The cross was, in fact, the full expression of the world's feeling toward Him. "There," they seemed to say, "Son of God, this is the manner in which God Himself should be treated, could we reach Him." Finally, the title of honor was nominally "King of the Jews," but that the blinded nation distinctly repudiated, and really called Him "King of thieves," by preferring Barabbas, and by placing Jesus in the place of highest shame between two thieves. His glory was thus in all things turned into shame by the sons of men.[3]

True honor, however, is His today; and universal sovereignty will yet be His in virtue of His thorns. May we give Him a true coronation and honor Him aright! Let us highly exalt Him in every part of our life! For His wounds, let us give Him worship; for His anguish, adoration; for His sobs, songs of adoration and praise.

3. Charles Spurgeon, *Morning and Evening* (New Kensington, PA: Whitaker House, 1997, 2002), 208.

HIS REDEMPTION

Several crowns are ours if we care to win them, and not one of them has a thorn entwined therein. Crowns without thorns can adorn our brows, seeing that Jesus was willing to wear a crown with thorns.

Salvation is ours because of the price the Master paid. His sacrifice is the only remedy for our sin, the inspiration of our present life, and the foundation of our future bliss. He was crowned with mockery in death, that we might be crowned with life everlasting.

Thorns and briars are the first product of the fall, and by wearing the crown of thorns He symbolized the bearing of the curse. Such a bloodstained diadem upon His brow indicated that the sin of the world garlanded His dear head and heart. He bore our sins in His own body up on the tree.

> Thy cruel thorns, Thy shameful cross
> Procure our heavenly crowns;
> Our highest gain springs from Thy loss;
> Our healing from Thy wounds.

HIS SOVEREIGNTY

As the result of that thorny crown worn so silently and bravely, Christ has gained eternal power over souls. His cross has become His throne. He sways our lives by His scars.

Those who murdered Him thought that they ended His claim as King, but they only added to His right to reign as the King of Kings. They thought that by placing a reed in His hands and then nailing it to a cross, they had taken the power from His palms. In effect, however, they relegated greater authority to those pierced hands of His.

They thought that by puncturing His holy heart with a thrust of the spear, the flow of love would be stayed, but such only added to the richness of the stream.

They believed that His greatness could be ended by placing Him within the tomb; but this last act only gave Him an opportunity to display His deathless power.

Christ now reigns from the tree. Those thorns capture our hearts. With sincerity we cry, "O Nazarene, Thou hast conquered our lives by Thine anguish!" His agonies, sufferings, and bloody sweat cause Him to take deep root in our affections. Enduring the cross, and despising the shame of it, He now rejoices as He witnesses the travail of His soul in your salvation and in mine.

The earthly life, gracious miracles and winning words of the Master will ever carry a charm; but He conquers us entirely by His dying love and outpoured blood upon the shameful cross! And love so amazing, so divine, demands and must have our soul, our life, our all.

Alas! however, men still give Him thorns. He can be crucified afresh.

> With thorns His temple gor'd and gash'd
> Send streams of blood from every part;
> His back's with knotted scourges lash'd.
> But sharper scourges tear His heart.

What are some of those sharp scourges tearing His loving heart in this far-off day? How can we grieve His tender Spirit? What thorns can we plat as a crown for His brow? Thorns! How can we distinguish them?

+ There is indifference to His suffering. O may we never lose the wonder and mystery of Calvary!

+ There is unbelief in His efficacious death. And this is the piercing sin of multitudes around. His anguish is nothing to them as they pass by.

+ There is the unreality of professed belief. May we be delivered from calling Him Lord and yet failing to do the things He commands!

+ There is inconsistency of life. What a thorn! And how it hurts the Master. Nothing is more painful for Him to bear.

+ There is the greed of worldly gain. How carnality grieves Him! Why, He died naked and was buried in a borrowed grave! He had nothing to leave but His clothes.

+ There is the neglect of others for whom He died. He feels it when we fail to reflect His passion. He stayed upon the cross that He might save others. Is His compassion ours?

Enough thorns were His on that dark day when they furrowed His brow—why give Him more? May our daily prayer be, "O Lord I would not willingly add to Thy sorrows. Help me to give Thee roses, instead of thorns!"

Joseph Plunkett, an Irish republican who died in 1916, wrote these beautiful lines:

> I see his blood upon the rose—
> And in the stars the glory of his eyes.
> His body gleams amid eternal snows,
> His tears fall from the skies.
>
> I see his face in every flower;
> The thunder and the singing of the birds
> Are but his voice;
> And carven by his power,
> Rocks are his written words.
>
> All pathways by his feet are worn;
> His strong heart stirs the ever-beating seas.
> His crown of thorns is twined with every thorn.
> His cross is every tree.[4]

---

4. Joseph Plunkett quoted in Kenneth E. Bailey, *Jesus Through Middle Eastern Eyes: Cultural Studies in the Gospels* (Downers Grove, IL: InterVarsity Press, 2008), 55.

3

THE MAN OF SORROWS

*"A man of sorrows…he hath borne our griefs,
and carried our sorrows.."*
—Isaiah 53:3–4

Isaiah's sad words drip with the red, royal blood of Jesus. What anguish they hold! And, who can ever plumb the tragic depths of His sorrows? One of the marvelous features of the fifty-third chapter of Isaiah is that you can break in at any point of it and preach a crucified Christ. It was thus that Philip used the chapter as he found the eunuch reading it.

The combination of the phrases before us indicates that Jesus became the man of sorrows through bearing our sorrows. Sorrows are common to man. They form his daily bread. And as sin, suffering, and death are the causes of all His sorrows, we may do well to consider the same in order to discover something of the load Jesus carried.

SIN

We all know something of this product of hell. Here is the force responsible for all the discord within and without, around and above. Sin is the root cause of distance and departure from God. It is the most horrible thing in the world, marring all that is beautiful. It is the source of all suffering and sorrow, trial and tragedy, darkness and death. And none are without its bane. *"All we like sheep have gone astray"* (Isaiah 53:6). Whether or not we believe it, *"all have sinned, and come short of the glory of God"* (Romans 3:23).

SUFFERING

The world is a house of suffering, as the result of sin. Suffering is a universal fact. Even nature herself, which does not appear to suffer, is man's companion in grief. *"The whole creation groaneth and travaileth in pain"* (Romans 8:22). With ears tuned to listen, we can detect a pang in her gladdest scene. As spring scatters her first wild flowers, we hear the scream of the rabbit as it is caught by the stoat or weasel. From the blue summer sky, the eagle sometimes sweeps down on pastureland and carries off a tender lamb from the fold. Beneath the calm, serene surface of the lake there struggles the minnow to escape out of the mouth of the pike.

If nature, therefore, has her pangs, losses, and sufferings, how much more a world of human lives. Jesus Himself found the world dripping with tears—tears to which His own were added. And if His eyes were red and wet with weeping, do not delude your heart into thinking that you will be able to escape the sharp thorns of suffering. Man is born to sorrow as the sparks fly upward! Today we have our songs, tomorrow our sighs. Today a crown of reception, tomorrow a cross of rejection.

DEATH

James reminds us that *"sin, when it is finished, bringeth forth death"* (James 1:15). What a cruel climax! Death, spiritual, physical, and eternal, is the inevitable outcome of all sin and suffering. These, then, are man's three sorrows—sin, suffering, death. And Christ became the Man of Sorrows seeing that He took these elements of sorrow and made them His own.

HE TOOK OUR SIN

The crowning point of Christ's sorrow was that, knowing no sin, He yet underwent a conscious incorporation with it. He who knew no sin was made sin for us. (See 2 Corinthians 5:21.) Made sin! Not made a sinner but made that ugly thing that produces all sinners. Without violence or deceit. (See Isaiah 53:9.) He yet became our sin-offering. (See verse 10.) Perfectly holy, He yet bore the sins of many and the iniquity of all. (See Isaiah 53:6, 12.) Without stain, He was yet numbered with the transgressors. (See verse 12.) And being made sin for us, Jesus underwent the sentence of eating sorrow all the days of His life. (See Genesis 3:17.)

> O make me understand it,
> Help me to take it in,
> What it meant to Thee,
> The Holy One,
> To bear away my sin.[5]

The sorrows of the Savior were unique in that they were unmeasured by any personal deviation from God. Absolute faultlessness was His. Thus His grief was what, as the Spotless One, He endured for others. In his epistle to the Roman senate concerning Jesus, Lentulus said, "He was never known to laugh." Worn with continual anguish over man's sin, He was taken for fifty when He was but thirty years of age. (See John 8:57.) Suffering was His intimate acquaintance, and the fellowship was sustained until the end. The load Jesus carried was heavy, yet He trudged every mile of the bloodred way until He cried in triumph, "*It is finished*" (John 19:30).

HE TOOK OUR DEATH

Isaiah reminds us that Jesus' body was buried in a rich man's grave. (See Isaiah 53:9.) The margin has it "*deaths.*" Deaths! How many deaths did He die? Why, He tasted death for every man. Can the human mind conceive it? The deaths of every person who has died, and will yet die, were rolled together into one death, which is known as "*the death of the cross*" (Philippians 2:8). All the waves and billows dashed against Jesus without cause. But willingly He bared His breast to the storm, for redemption for the sinner could come in no other way. He knew that

> The path of sorrow, and that path alone,
> Leads to the land where sorrow is unknown.[6]

---

5. Katharine A. M. Kelly, "Oh, Make Me Understand It."
6. William Cowper, "An Epistle to an Afflicted Protestant Lady in France."

And in His loving condescension, He made His weary feet tread that rugged path leading as it did up Calvary's slope.

We are now ready for an examination of the poignant phrase "Man of Sorrows"!

CHRIST WAS...

1. "A MAN..." (ISAIAH 53:3).

One is grateful that the prophet Isaiah expressed it thus. Had it read, "A God of Sorrows," perhaps it would not have carried the same appeal. And yet He was God as well as Man. Said a brilliant German sceptic to a Christian, "If I could see what your God sees, I would break my heart." The Christian replied, "At the cross, God's heart did break." When God came down to deliver Israel from Egypt, He said to Moses, "*I know their sorrows*" (Exodus 3:7). And it takes a God to understand the sorrows of men.

> There is no place where earth's sorrows
> Are more felt than up in heaven.[7]

And the glory of the incarnation is that God came down from the Ivory Palaces and became a Man, sin excepted; and in this manner, He not only knew our sorrows but made them His own. Becoming Man, He understood life from man's standpoint. And it is this vision of the Master which inspires hearts that suffer. The thought of a suffering Christ enables man to bear his load.

Thus we see Jesus, not tasting human joys, but drinking the dregs of the cup of human grief. There was no sorrow like unto His. He spoke of His soul as being troubled and exceedingly sorrowful. And we must not associate Him as the Man of Sorrows with the last scene of His life, tragic as it was. His whole life was

> One continued chain
> Of labour, sorrow, and consuming pain.[8]

7. Frederick W. Faber, "There's a Wideness in God's Mercies," 1854.
8. Sir R. Blackmore.

His sorrows, however, never robbed Him of His peace or of His confidence in God. They only intensified His faith. When His grief reached its greatest intensity, He did not allow it to deter Him from His great task. His sorrows were borne without complaint, and in this, He has left us an example that we should follow. No wonder we sing, "Man of Sorrows, what a name!"[9]

2. "...OF SORROWS" (ISAIAH 53:3).

There was no bitter cup Christ did not taste as He lived among men. He suffered Himself to be tested *"in all points...like as we are"* (Hebrews 4:15).

> In every pang that rends the heart
> The Man of Sorrows had a part.[10]

And none will ever be able to realize all that He endured as He tasted all kinds of sorrow, trial, and adversity. We shall never know

> How dark was the night the Lord passed through
> Ere He found His sheep that was lost.[11]

His Sorrows Were Internal

The sorrows Christ carried were internal—sorrows of heart, mind, soul, and spirit; sorrows too deep for us to understand. How the holy nature of Jesus must have writhed in torture under what He saw, heard, and felt. We are told that, *"looking up to heaven,* [Jesus] *sighed"* (Mark 7:34). Alas! this was His constant attitude. Life for Him was one long sigh, a drawn-out sob.

His Sorrows Were Fraternal

Again, the sorrows He endured were those that leaped upon His heart as He came into contact with those among whom He lived and

9. Philip Paul Bliss, "Hallelujah! What a Savior," 1875.
10. Michael Bruce, "Where High the Heavenly Temple Stands," 1781.
11. Elizabeth C. Clephane, "The Ninety and Nine," 1868.

labored. Away from the Father's home, He was a stranger in the world and was always made to know and feel it. From childhood, He had thoughts He could not utter. Had He done so, they would have never been understood by His closest friends. But it is His fraternal sorrow that makes Him dear to our hearts. He mingled His tears with those of the sorrowing friends of Lazarus. (See John 11:35.) He wept over the sins of a city. (See Luke 19:41.) His heart was moved with compassion as He looked out upon the multitudes. (See Matthew 9:36.)

O for more fraternal sorrow! We do not have hearts that feel for others. We are so cold, so selfish, so heartless. The sorrows of earth do not move us to tears and prayers for the lost. God, give us Calvary hearts!

His Sorrows Were Paternal

In Isaiah's chapter of the cross, he has a phrase somewhat hard to understand. He tells us that it pleased the Lord to bruise His Son. *"It pleased the* Lord *to bruise him"* (Isaiah 53:10). Thus, in a deep, unfathomable way, sorrow was placed upon Him by the hand of His loving Father above. His crown of sorrows was when God made Christ to be sin for others. (See 2 Corinthians 5:21.) And as a Son, He learned obedience by the things He suffered. And such God-placed sorrow reached its climax when Jesus cried, *"My God, my God, why hast thou forsaken me?"* (Matthew 27:46; Mark 15:34).

But is it not blessed to know that the darkest day in His experience was for Him a revenue of gladness and a harvest of eternal praise? His sorrows give Him souls. Every new life entering His kingdom causes Him fresh delight and joy. With every soul saved, He sees of the travail of His soul and is satisfied. His church is a blessed harvest of tears.

Have you praised Him for His anguish of soul and laceration of body and shedding of blood? May you pray with others—

O King of suffering and sorrow! Monarch of the marred face, none has ever approached thee in the extremity of thy grief. We bow the knee, and bid thee "All Hail!" We are conquered by thy tears and woes.

Our hearts are enthralled; our souls inspired; our lives surrendered to thy disposal for the execution of purposes which cost thee so dear.[12]

If you represent the fruit of His suffering, then, if called upon to live as a man or woman of sorrow, you can rely upon the companionship of Him who trod the bloodred way before you.

12. F. B. Meyer, *Christ in Isaiah* (Fort Washington, PA: CLC Publications, 2013).

4

GODFORSAKEN

"My God, my God, why hast thou forsaken me?"
—Matthew 27:46; Mark 15:34

Seven times Jesus spoke from the cross, and the poignant question before us constituted His fourth cry. What such an utterance means is too deep and mysterious to explain! We can only think of the words with hushed hearts. They must be approached with reverence, for the place whereon we stand is holy ground.

There we behold the Savior in the depth of His sorrows, for the cry indicates the black midnight of His terror. At this moment, physical weakness was united with acute torture arising from the shame and ignominy through which He was to pass. The world, of course, had been prepared for such a cry, seeing that it had commenced the Calvary Psalm, where His agonies were foretold with such exactness. (See Psalm 22.) This fourth saying from Jesus on the cross indicates the bitterest drop in His bitter cup.

"MY GOD, MY GOD"

Throughout the Passion Week, Jesus had borne His inexpressible agony in sublime silence of soul. Now that this climax was reached, He gave vent to such a heartrending cry. Martin Luther says that the verse suggests "God forsaken by God." And the repetition speaks of the depth of anguish Jesus must have felt.

Truly the cross presents strange contrasts. Hands stretched forth in blessing for man were now outstretched upon a cross, mangled and torn by those they had blessed. Feet that had trodden no forbidden pathway, but which were ever active on errands of mercy, were now so cruelly pierced. The brow upon which the dove of peace had rested was now encircled with thorns, the symbol of sin. Lips into which grace had been poured and out of which gracious words had flowed were now the parched lips of a lonely Sufferer, crying, *"My God, my God, why hast thou forsaken me?"* (Matthew 27:46; Mark 15:34).

It will be noted that Jesus did not say "Father" as in His first cry and also in His last, but He said, *"My God."* He usually addressed God as "Father," but here He said *"God,"* for He appealed to divine Righteousness. Somewhere in the darkness, He felt pushed out of the Father's heart and as if He was in a desolate forest. Yet He clung to divine Righteousness. In spite of the mystery of the moment, He knew that God as God must have been doing right.

It is also a blessing to realize how faith can cling to God in the dark. Although Jesus could not see God's face, He still called Him *"**My** God."* There was extreme trust in extreme trial! And it is somewhat remarkable that He used the Syrian word for God, "Eloi," so His cry can be translated, "My Strength, my Strength!" Crucified in weakness, He required the strength of the mighty One, hence His cry.

If somehow we lose sight of His countenance, may this be our attitude. In the hour of darkness, may we lay hold of His strength. As we pass through inexplicable experiences and it seems as if the Father's smile has been eclipsed by the clouds, may we, with a desperate faith, learn to sing,

> Thou know'st my soul does dearly love
> The place of Thy abode;
> No music drops so sweet a sound
> As these two words, *My God!*[13]

---

13. Thomas Shepherd quoted in *The Gospel Standard, or Feeble Christian's Support*, vol. 48 (London: Temple Printing Works, 1882), 171.

"WHY?"

This is the only time Christ's heart was filled with wonder concerning what His Father had allowed. And perhaps an answer to His question can be found in Psalm 22:3, *"But thou art holy."* Jesus was on the cross as the representation of sinful humanity. As one writer expressed it,

> He gazed across the awful gulf through which He must wade, He looked down into the horrible pit in whose depths He must struggle and up whose insurmountable sides He must painfully climb with bleeding hands and feet. He saw sins, sins, sins, pressing in upon His holy body from this side and that, from behind, before, and above, and knew that as the Sin-Bearer He must bear them all and so He was left alone—alone with human sin, with your sin and mine.

The face of the Father turned not so much away from Christ as from what He was bearing, namely, the load of the world's sin, which ultimately broke Christ's loving, compassionate heart. He was there on the plane of sinners with mountains upon mountains of guilt encircling Him, thus the Father hid His face from such a horrible load, seeing that He was of purer eyes than to behold evil.

We dishonor Christ if we think that some of His cries in Gethsemane and Calvary were only moans of anguish stimulated by a natural fear of death. Thousands of His followers have faced a death equally as cruel with quietness of resignation and a spirit of victory, with no cry whatever escaping their lips. But at His death, Jesus was not dying as a martyr; He was tasting the bitter cup of every life, and facing the mystery of sin-bearing.

And such a cry makes Him our Brother in mystery. There is a "why" in every life. Some have stood at the side of an empty cradle and have asked, "Why?" Others with blasted hopes, blighted friendships, and broken vows have asked, "Why?"

The Sunday after Dr. Joseph Parker, of the City Temple, had buried his beautiful wife, his congregation wondered what text he would preach upon. He chose the one before us and said, "I thank God there was a 'why' in the Savior's life." Yes, and such a fact brings comfort amid our loneliness and desolation.

Have you reached a Calvary? Do you feel as if the Lord has left you? O thou poor, distressed and seemingly Godforsaken one, if in darkness, the Father is still with thee! Cling to Him! Trust Him even though you cannot trace Him.

Yes, we live in a world of whys and wherefores. What God permits we know not now; but we shall know hereafter. If presently you see darkly through a glass, you must be patient, for the paradise of revelation is ahead. If, like your Lord, you are being made to suffer although you are innocent of what is being laid at your door, if your heart is torn by a sorrow some unkind hand is responsible for, you must realize that you are not alone. Jesus is your Brother in adversity. Although the innocent One, and nearer to God's heart than any other has ever been, He yet cried, "*Why…?*"

> The scourge, the thorns, the deep disgrace,
> These Thou couldst bear, nor once repine;
> But when Jehovah veiled His face,
> Unutterable pangs were Thine.[14]

"FORSAKEN"

What a tragic word! We seem to hear the moan of a broken heart within it. To forsake means to leave behind in any state or place. And the word leaving the lips of Jesus, as it did, conveys the idea of desertion. What a term to come from One who was bathed in the sunshine of His loving Father's presence! The nails in His flesh, the insult of His enemies, the shame of the cross, the cruelty of men, did not cause anything like the grief Christ experienced when, for the time being, He seemed to lose the sense of His Father's presence. As He walked among men, in spite of their hostility, He could say, "*I am not alone, because the Father is with me*" (John 16:32). But here He is apparently abandoned by God.

---

14. John W. Cunningham, "From Calvary a Cry Was Heard," 1824.

The darkness of earth, then, was in keeping with the darkness that hung over the Redeemer's spirit as He was Godforsaken. There was darkness around, darkness within, but worst of all, darkness above, seeing that God's face was hidden.

The crowning crime of man [was] the crime of killing the Prince of Life…[thereby] casting out the Lord of Nature from His own world.[15]

And such a crime may not be allowed to pass without some protest from Nature herself, hence midday was turned to midnight. Denser darkness, however, came with God's withdrawal.

Is darkness abounding in your life at this moment? Do you wonder whether God is near, or whether He hears your cry? Have you been left forsaken, deserted, betrayed? If close, creep closer to your Lord and listen to His voice echoing down the corridor of your being—"*I will never leave thee, nor forsake thee*" (Hebrews 13:5). Jesus was forsaken in His lone hour that He might have grace to tell you that He will be with you for always, even unto the end of the road.

"ME"

What poignant grief this personal pronoun carries!

Yes, "*Me*" above all others. Me! Thy well-beloved Son. I have always done the things pleasing to Thee. I ever glorified Thee on earth. I was the One in whom Thou delighted. Why, why hast Thou left Me alone to bear this bitter load? Surely there has never been such a long, lonely cry from earth as the one from the cross. "*Why hast thou forsaken me?*" It was a cry of surprise, of consternation, the irrepressible cry of a life tried to its utmost limit of possibility. What a mystery! We cannot fathom it. We know only that for one brief moment, it seemed as if Jesus was forsaken by His Father, that He was left alone to die.

Possibly this pronoun is an echo of your heart's experience. You find yourself saying, "Why has God treated *me* this way? I have ever

---

15. Charles Stanford, *Voices from Calvary: A Course of Homilies* (London: The Religious Tract Society, 1881), 161.

striven to live a holy, separated life. I have loved His Word, His house, and His people. My life and substance have ever been at His disposal, so why does He treat me thus? Lord, what have I done? I can understand a sinner suffering, for he is but reaping the harvest of his evil deeds; but Lord, why hast Thou allowed this heavy cross to fall upon my shoulders?" Sorrowing, perplexed heart, the Master has not left you alone, for He has promised never to forsake you. (See Deuteronomy 31:6.) Never mistake feelings for actualities. If indwelt by His Spirit, then you can never be deserted, for the God above will never forsake the God within you. The Holy Spirit is your "perpetual Comforter" and "eternal Inhabitant," as Saint Augustine called Him.

Yea, once, Immanuel's orphaned cry His universe hath shaken—
It went up single, echoless, "My God, I am forsaken!"

It went up from the Holy's lips amid His lost creation,
That, of the lost, no son should use those words of desolation![16]

---

16. Elizabeth Barrett Browning, "Cowper's Grave."

5

A CRIMSON WORD

"The blood of Jesus."
—Hebrews 10:19

There is no word as distasteful and repugnant to the proud heart of man as the crimson word *blood*. Deep revulsion arises within the mind of those who are refined yet not regenerated as they listen to a preacher exalting the precious blood, or as blood-hymns are sung. Such scorn and contempt over this dyed-red word are unnecessary when it is remembered that it is a solemn and appealing figure, a concrete and pictorial expression, of a glorious truth. The Hebrew word for *"blood"* described a sacrifice—the East being more expressive than the West.

The Bible, it will be noted, is a crimson Book. It is saturated with blood and permeated with the message and method of redemption. Men may sneer at a book so gory, at a word as crimson as *blood*; but to those who, like John, have experienced its cleansing efficacy, there is nothing save glory in its ruby brilliance. As Moses sprinkled Israel's partial Bible with blood, so the whole Bible and the Christian church are sprinkled with blood.

THE SUPREME SACRIFICE OF THE SINLESS SUBSTITUTE

Within the New Testament, there are three pictorial phrases and phases describing the supreme sacrifice of the sinless Substitute for sinners.

THE DEATH OF CHRIST

When the Word speaks *thus*, it takes us to Calvary and shows us Jesus crowning His life with the supreme deed and achievement of His death. He came into the world to save sinners; and through His death, salvation was achieved.

THE CROSS OF CHRIST

Again, our feet are guided to the most sacred spot on earth, this time to think of the physical agonies of the Savior. Such a phrase likewise reminds us of the curse pronounced upon sin, which curse Jesus bore when He hung upon the tree.

THE BLOOD OF CHRIST

Here we have the outpouring of the Sufferer Himself. *"The life of the flesh is in the blood"* (Leviticus 17:11). The value of a life is, in measure, the value of the blood. May the Holy Spirit enable us to penetrate all that is wrapped up in the crimson word, as we now come to examine it!

THE CHARACTER OF THE BLOOD

We are so constituted that nothing is so affecting as the crimson blood flowing from a person. Instinctively, we recoil from the sight of liquid life as it gushes forth. What feelings grip your heart as you gaze upon the suspended Victim of the cross? Are you moved to tears of contrition as you behold Christ's torn body and the blood oozing from His wounds, gathering in a pool at His sacred feet?

The blood He shed that day was from no poor, mean, weak, vitiated man. Rather, was it unique in its value and inherent nature, hence its perpetual efficacy.

PHASES OF MURDER IN CHRIST'S CRUCIFIXION

Of course, there are various ways of viewing the darkest blot upon the pages of history. When cruel men murdered Jesus by hanging Him on a tree, they were guilty of various phases of murder. Suicide is the murder of self; homicide, the murder of man; fratricide, the murder of a brother; patricide, the murder of a father; regicide, the murder of a king; deicide, the murder of a god.

SUICIDE, THE MURDER OF ONESELF

Judas, the traitor, haunted by his own black sin, died by his own hand. In the Field of Blood, he placed himself upon a tree and took his life. (See Matthew 27:5.) He that commits suicide takes his life; Jesus gave His life. It is true that He was taken and slain and hanged upon a tree by wicked men, yet He could have stayed the murderous intentions of the Jews. Having power to lay down His life, He allowed it to be taken. He chose the place of His death and fixed its hour. *"Mine hour is not yet come"* (John 2:4). It cannot be that a prophet perish out of Jerusalem. There was a sense, then, in which He shed His own blood, seeing that His life was given, not taken. He gave Himself up to the cross. And we are bound to regard a suicidal action of this sort as immoral if it is actuated by any other motive than that of the "greater love which lays down its life for its friend." (See John 15:13.)

HOMICIDE, THE MURDER OF A MAN

When Moses slew the Egyptian, he was guilty of homicide. (See Exodus 2:12.) Appealing to the pity of the crowd, Pilate cried, *"Behold the man!"* (John 19:5). And Christ was certainly the fairest, purest specimen of manhood the world has ever gazed upon. But although Christ was fairer than the children of men, the crowd cried, *"Crucify him, crucify him"* (Luke 23:21). Then the sword awoke against our fellow. (See Zechariah 13:7.) Humanity slew its perfect Representative. Man murderously slew its own Kinsman, the Man Christ Jesus.

FRATRICIDE, THE MURDER OF A BROTHER

The early dawn of the human race provides us with a tragic illustration of this type of murder—in Abel's slaying of his brother, Cain. (See Genesis 4:8.) If one saw an entire stranger being maltreated and his life being battered out, he would certainly feel indignant and seek to help the ill-treated one. But suppose it was discovered that villains were beating the life out of his own brother; certainly the suffering of his own blood would stir him to the depths. At the peril of losing his own life, he would rush in and willingly fight to the death in an effort to save his own flesh. As blood is thicker than water, ill-treatment of a brother deeply affects another member of the same family.

Now, Calvary witnessed the death of our elder Brother. What are your emotions as you hear of the blood of Christ, knowing that it was the blood of One who was bone of your bone and flesh of your flesh? Do you feel that if had you been there, with supernatural power you would have rushed the mob and, drawing the nails from His hands and feet, lifted His limp, bloodstained frame off the cross, then seek the shelter of some loving home to nurse Him back to health? Would you have made an effort to scatter His foes as they maltreated Him by spitting upon His face, tearing out His hair, and brutally insulting Him and exposing Him to such shameful indignities?

Ah, let the truth be told! It was your sin that slew your elder Brother. Your iniquities were responsible for Calvary's crime of fratricide. His blood is on your hands. Well might you cry with Pilate for water to erase such a terrible stain! (See Matthew 27:24.) The only place, however, where one can rid himself of the foul murder of God's Son and man's Brother born for adversity is in the fountain opened for all sin and uncleanness. (See Zechariah 13:1.)

PATRICIDE, THE MURDER OF A FATHER

Surely there is nothing as callous and despicable as the slaughter of one's own parent. Yet the cross presents us with patricide, seeing that Christ was the everlasting Father. At the cross, man killed the kindest, most fatherly heart the world ever knew. And in spite of sin, Christ still waits to be a Father unto us. While Jesus was the true Son of His Father, the personification of His Father's love, and the culmination of the revelation of the Father, He yet stands out as the Father of the redeemed. When the red blood flowed from His wounds, it oozed forth from one of the most fatherly hearts that loved and cared for mankind.

REGICIDE, THE MURDER OF A KING

This glaring crime of the anarchist finds many illustrations in history, both sacred and secular. In these days of communism, crowns and thrones sometimes perish overnight.

The blood of Jesus was of intrinsic value, seeing that it was royal blood. Born a King, Jesus died as one! Thus His name indicated His cross—Jesus, King of the Jews! What widespread grief there is when a nation wakes up one morning and reads "The King has been murdered!" When Jesus died, He shed the blood with the health and royalty of the King of Kings within it. He suffered on the cross as the King, crucified.

This is why one is condemned if he tramples underfoot the blood of the everlasting covenant. It is the blood of the King immortal, invisible, and eternal. And the exalted nature of the blood adds to the sinner's guilt and condemnation as he spurns it. Lordship and kingship give Christ's blood inconceivable value.

> Alas, and did my Savior bleed,
> And did my Sovereign die![17]

DEICIDE, THE MURDER OF A GOD

After the murder of the czar of Russia, and the extermination of others of royal blood, the Bolsheviks issued a cartoon representing one of their number with a bloody axe in hand, climbing a ladder extending to heaven. The caption of the coarse picture was "And now for God!" And the paganism sweeping the world today is out to murder God.

Paul has no scruples in calling the blood of Jesus the blood of God. (See Acts 20:28.) It is certainly true that it was unmistakably human blood that felt the horrors and agonies of the cross as only perfect humanity could. The miracle, however, of the incarnation was the fusion of deity and humanity into one personality. Thus, when Jesus died, He shed the blood not only of Mary's Son but of One who was the mighty God. Calvary presents the death of the Creator dying by the hand of the creature, for the creature's sins.

17. Isaac Watts, "Alas, and Did My Savior Bleed," 1707.

And this is why the blood is unspeakably precious and can make the foulest clean. It was the blood of God yet Man; of the King yet Servant; of the Shepherd yet Lamb; of the Priest yet Sacrifice. What a profound mystery! This is why, if we reject the blood, it would have been better had we never been born. (See Matthew 26:24.)

THE CLEANSING OF THE BLOOD

John extolled the virtue of the blood to wash, or loose, him from his sin. Are we certain that we have been washed in the blood of the Lamb? It would seem as if the New Testament observes four related methods of cleansing.

1. CLEANSING BY WATER

The rite of baptism portrays all that is involved in the work of the Holy Spirit on the basis of the cross. The new birth within the soul is the operation of the Spirit, who is often symbolized as water. (See John 3:5; Ephesians 5:26.)

2. CLEANSING BY THE WORD

Water is likewise a symbol of the Word. (See John 15:3.) As we read the Scriptures, as we hear them proclaimed, the truth pierces our innermost being like a sword. Sin is seen in the white light of God's countenance, and we are driven to the source of cleansing. What the light reveals, the blood cleanses! Thus the Word cleanses in that it sends us to the riven wounds of Jesus.

3. CLEANSING BY FIRE

Secretly, swiftly, mysteriously, the Spirit descends upon all that is base and foul, consuming such in His fiery flame. And our own desires to serve the Christ who died for us are quickened by the Spirit of burning.

4. CLEANSING BY BLOOD

This is the gentlest, tenderest, and most powerful of all modes of purification. Christ's actual blood, of course, no longer exists. Cleansing by blood means that in virtue of His death, Jesus can cleanse and save. And His blood, so freely shed, cries either for salvation or condemnation. If you accept Christ, then His blood cries out for your pardon. And as God sees the blood protecting you, He passes over you. If, however, the blood is rejected, then it cries out for condemnation. Despised, it pleads against the sinner. Throughout eternity, the gaping wounds of Christ haunt the soul with the thought of the healing balm they could have imparted.

Dwight L. Moody used to tell the story of the days when the gold fever swept California. A man went West leaving his wife and their boy in New England. Soon, he succeeded and sent for his dear ones. His wife's heart leaped for joy. Taking her boy to New York, she boarded a Pacific steamer sailing for San Francisco. The ship, however, had not been out at sea before there was the cry "Fire! Fire!" Onboard was a powder magazine, and the Captain knew that the moment the fire reached the store, all would perish. Lifeboats were crowded with people, but they proved to be too small and few. As the last boat pushed away, the mother pled with the boatman to take her and the boy.

"No, I dare not take another. If I do, we will all sink," was his reply.

Earnestly, the woman continued to plead, and, at last, the boatman consented to take one more person. Do you think the mother leaped into the boat, leaving her boy to perish with others? No, she seized him, gave him one last hug, and dropped him into the boat, with the wail "My boy, if you live to see your father, tell him that I died in your place."

And if he did live, do you think that he would speak contemptuously of his mother, who went down into a watery grave for him?

Jesus died in your place. Your sins deserved eternal death. But Jesus died your death and bore your curse. Have you received Him as Savior? Do you love Him? Are you sheltered in His wounded side? Listen to the music of the gospel: *"Though your sins be as scarlet, they shall be as white as snow; though they be red like crimson, they shall be as wool"* (Isaiah 1:18).

If uncleansed, plunge now into the crimson flood and thereby join the multitudes no man can number, who extol the blood for having washed and loosed them from their sin.

6

THE CALVARY DOXOLOGY

"Unto him that loved us,
and washed us from our sins in his own blood."
—Revelation 1:5

The New Testament knows no gospel save the one scorned by many seemingly religious people as well as by the openly godless. It is the death of the Lord Jesus Christ upon the rugged cross. His superb sacrifice eclipses all other themes in the appeals of the Epistles. Millions upon earth and in glory who have experienced the pardon, purity, and peace of the cross, with united breath,

> Ascribe their conquest to the Lamb,
> Their triumph to His death.[18]

THE CLEANSING BLOOD OF CHRIST

The noble army of men and women who have hazarded their lives at home and abroad for His dear sake have all alike been actuated by the passion of the cross. It is therefore without apology that we turn again to the blessed theme of the blood of the world's Redeemer and coming King. Now we will discuss how His blood operates as a cleansing factor in the lives of sinners, to which class we all belong.

IT REVEALS THE TRUE NATURE OF SIN

It was Dr. Edward Bouverie Pusey who said, "The sun never sets on sin." How true! Sin is the most evident yet dreadful fact in life. Because

18. Isaac Watts, "Give Me the Wings of Faith," 1709.

of our relationship to our first parents, we are born with an evil nature and an inborn love of evil. (See Psalm 51:5.) Developing physically, we pass from being sinners by birth to sinners by practice.

Sin comes to us clothed in light, radiant with charm, and marked with beauty. At the time, we do not look behind its features to see the devil, the hellish parent of sin. It is after we have sinned that we realize how deluded we have been. The moment after the mask is torn off, we discover how hideous a thing sin is. Because the cross unmasks sin's true nature, it is possible to have such a revelation the moment before committal by looking up at the marred face of Jesus. If we could see the leering eyes of the Tempter as he approaches us in some form of sin, we would never fall into his snare.

Let us mark how the sacrifice of Calvary exposes the sin of those who sit beneath its shadow.

The traitor-deed of Judas is made thrice despicable, horrible, and callous as the pure, white light of the cross is focused upon it.

The gross and debauched spirit of Herod stands revealed in all its nakedness in the sight of the crucified Savior he helped to murder.

The cowardly heart of Pilate, the man lacking the courage of his convictions, is made more visible alongside the bloody cross he helped erect.

The sin of your heart and mine is blacker still when we bring it to that hill, lone and gray, upon which God's Holy One died.

Let us turn that searching light of His sacrifice upon the life we live in order to recoil from the forbidden things we presently love.

Ill temper, petty pride, empty vanity, worldliness—how we recoil in shame from these works of the flesh as we lift them up in the light of His dear cross. We can never view His five bleeding wounds without discovering some fresh aspect of sin's diabolical nature. If we have any doubt about a habit, the cross is ever the acid test of validity.

The story is told of three students traveling in Roman Catholic parts of Switzerland. With all the self-importance of youth, they deemed their godly homes, in which they had been trained, somewhat rigid and narrow. In student life, they smiled at prayer and scorned the godly ways of praying parents.

During their travels, however, they came to a rudely shaped cross on the wayside, and at the foot of it lay a few cheap offerings placed there by poor women of a nearby village. At the sight of the cross, silence fell upon the three students. Light somehow was cast upon their evil deeds, and their hearts were revealed. In a moment, they *saw* their sinfulness and confessed their transgressions as they bowed before the wayside cross. Likewise, our iniquity can be purged, and the horribleness of our sin made clear, only by the sight of the wondrous cross on which the Prince of Glory died.

This is how the life of the one penning these lines was arrested well over a quarter of a century ago, and was thus diverted from its emptiness, frivolity, and uselessness into a purer, nobler channel. My eyes once feasted upon the sight so dazzling in *Vanity Fair*. My young heart was charmed as I spent time and money in theaters and music halls. But one night within the house of God, my vision was directed to the greatest drama ever acted upon the world's stage, namely, the bitter death of God's fairest and best. A vision of the bloodred feet of Jesus trudging up the stone-hewn hill of Calvary turned my feet to God's testimonies. An inveterate smoker, I came to see that nicotine-stained fingers did not correspond to the pierced hands of Jesus. Such hands, I felt, would never handle betting slips, cards, and trashy novels; thus, many worldly pleasures went. Dancing slippers, I came to see, could never adorn and befit the torn, bleeding feet of the Man of Calvary.

Of course, the unconverted are not asked to surrender their glittering toys and much-loved pleasures. A spiritual disposition is the first necessity, and this comes through the reception of Christ as Savior. Worldlings are sometimes perturbed by what they must give up if they become Christians. The first word of the gospel, however, is not "give" but "receive." (See John 1:12.)

God's people are on a different level. Entrance into the kingdom may be free, but once in, the Lord demands all we have. Thus, if you are a Christian and find yourself troubled about various forms of worldly pleasure, you must seek out some quiet corner and, falling before the sacred, bleeding form of Jesus, lay the pursuits you have a doubt about at the foot of His cross. Ask the blood-stained Man of Calvary how to deal with your tobacco, cards, and passion for the movies, dance, and other kindred amusements. Ask Him what He means by being crucified unto the world and having the world crucified unto you (see Galatians 6:14), and He will not fail to answer you.

IT UNFOLDS THE LOVE OF GOD

It is sadly possible for the highest and most beautiful life not to touch some hearts, impelling them to a nobler life. Judas left the Lord's Table when he had gazed upon the face of Sorrow and had heard His final appeal of love, to seal the fatal bargain. Many a son has lived in a home surrounded by a father's prayers and a mother's sanctity and has yet passed out into the haunts of sin.

But there is nothing that so shames a sinner for his unfaithfulness and sin, and inspires him to live for the highest, like the revelation of the love of God. The mighty power that compels him to follow the light is the long-suffering of God. Looking up at the cross, he realizes that it reflects a divine love the many waters of rejection cannot quench, and he is conquered thereby. As a result of such a vision, there passes through the heart a deep penitence issuing in a full surrender to the Crucified One.

A classic illustration of the power of God's love as manifested in Christ's sacrifice to cleanse from sin is that to be found in the life of Captain Hedley Vicars of the West Indian Army. As a youth, he was blameless. Having come early under religious influences, he passed into his regiment a man with high moral standards. He was religious but had not yet been saved.

One day, however, the truth of the love of God as revealed in the cross flashed in upon his heart, and he came to experience the deep cleansing of the blood. Here is the record of Hedley Vicar's change of heart as given by his biographer:

It was in the month of Nov., 1851, that while waiting the return of a brother officer in his room, he idly turned over the leaves of a Bible which lay on the table. The words caught his eye "The blood of Jesus Christ, His son, cleanseth us from all sin." Closing the book he said, "If this be true for me, henceforth I will live by the grace of God, as a man should live, who has been washed in the blood of Jesus Christ."...The past, he said, then, is blotted out, what I have to do is to go forward; I cannot return to the sins from which my Saviour has cleansed me with his blood."[19]

My sinner friend, the cross tells you that no matter how you have sinned, God loves you and He waits to emancipate you from the thralldom of your sin.

> God loves you—
> His Word proclaims it.
> The Cross reveals it.
> The Spirit declares it.

Will you accept it and rest in the fact of His love forever?

IT REMOVES OUR INIQUITIES

What a priceless jewel of divine revelation is John's word about the blood having efficacy to cleanse the sinner from *all* sin! (See 1 John 1:7.) We can be delivered, then, from the shackles of sin not by our own self-effort or self-righteousness, good deeds, churchgoing, prayers, and religious acts, but only by the shed blood of Christ.

> This is all my hope and peace,
> Nothing but the blood of Jesus.[20]

If one is without guile, like Nathanael, he must die without hope unless the shelter of the blood is sought. On his dying bed, an aged minister said

---

19. Catherine Marsh, *A Sketch of the Life of Capt. Hedley Vicars, the Christian Soldier* (Richmond: Macfarlane & Fergusson, 1862), 6.
20. Robert Lowry, "Nothing but the Blood of Jesus," 1876.

to those around him, "Bring me the Bible." When he had it in his hands, he placed his finger on the verse containing the Calvary Doxology and confessed, "I die in hope of this verse." He knew that it was not his good life or fifty years' preaching but absolute dependence upon the blood of Jesus Christ that would bear him over the dark waters of death.

OTHER CHARACTERISTICS OF THE BLOOD OF CHRIST

After the initial cleansing in the hour of regeneration, we need to be cleansed again and again from the defilement of sin. Let us now look at some unceasing gifts of the blood of Christ.

THE BLOOD HAS UNCEASING VIRTUE

Some cherish the blindest of all delusions that they are already perfect and have no further need of the cleansing blood. The majority of us, however, are only too conscious of the subtle attractions of the flesh and that there is a constant need, therefore, of the unceasing virtue of the crimson flood. If we would walk with undisturbed peace of heart, then we must bring our sin, whether small or great, to the blood as soon as we are made conscious of it. Short accounts with God ever mean a life of precious fellowship with Him.

THE BLOOD CARRIES UNLIMITED VICTORY

If one could marshal all the sins of a single life, the quantity would be horrifying. Eyes would close in disgust! There would be sins against God and man; sins against the Lord's Day and the sacraments; sins against body and soul; sins against light and knowledge; sins against Christ, the Spirit, the Bible, and the church; sins against loved ones and friends. Yet the declaration is that the blood can loose or wash us from all sin—all kinds and degrees. (See 1 John 1:7.) No matter how black, ugly, and horrible sin may have been, the blood poured out at Calvary contains sufficient efficacy to wash away every sin of every sinner the world over, if sinners will but repair to the fount of cleansing.

If the blood of Jesus was only the blood of a martyr who died for a truth he believed, then it carries no atoning power. But if His blood was that of a Savior dying for sinners, as we believe it was, then it can deliver from all sin. As the blood of a martyr, Christ's blood would carry no more value than the blood of Paul soaked in the dust as his head was severed from his body, or that of Hugh Latimer, simmering in the burning fire. But Christ's blood is different, seeing that it was the blood of God's holy Lamb.

Have you been guilty of sin, of the sin of robbery, murder, drunkenness, lust, swearing, of the finer sins of pride and self-righteousness? Well, bring the terrible load, heap it up as high as you can, and cause the cross to bear down upon it! The blood can snap the strongest fetter hell ever forged. It can make the foulest clean!

The story is told of a Roman Catholic who had never possessed a Bible. One day, he came across a copy which he and his wife read with great zest. As they read, the Holy Spirit brought home to their minds the truth of God's free salvation through the death of the Savior on the cross. "Wife," the man exclaimed, "if this Book is true, we are lost." Reading on, the glorious message of the cleansing of the blood became so real to him that he stopped and cried with rapture, "Wife, if this Book is true, we can be saved." And saved they were.

Yes, the crimson Book is true! Apart from Christ, man is lost, helpless, and hopeless. But the precious blood, sprinkling the sacred pages, tells man that no matter how many or mighty his sins may be, he can overcome them all, and the devil behind them, by the sacrifice of the Lord.

7

REIGNING FROM THE TREE

"The Lord reigneth from the tree."

Within the Psalter, we have eight royal Psalms. Psalms 93–100 are known as the theocratic Psalms, seeing that they portray various aspects of the kingdom of Jehovah. Psalm 96 is a great missionary Psalm revealing as it does Israel's responsibility to make Jehovah known among the nations. And emphasis was to be laid upon the world empire of the heavenly King. He was to be declared as Emperor. There is, of course, a distinction between king and emperor. A king is the chief ruler in and over a nation. An emperor, however, is the highest title of sovereignty and suggests a ruler of nations and of lesser sovereigns. The Lord, then, is a world Emperor, the King of Kings. And the day is coming when the kingdoms of this world will become His world kingdom, and He will reign supreme over all. (See Revelation 11:15.)

The verse before us forms the basic point of this missionary Psalm. Occupying, practically, the center of the Psalm, it is full of deep, spiritual import. Earthly kings reign and have thrones, and the Lord has His throne from which He rules.

Psalm 96:10 in our English version ends with *"the Lord reigneth."* An old Latin version, however, reads, "The Lord reigneth from the tree." Justin Martyr accused the Jews of erasing the words "from the tree" from the original because of their intense hatred of Christ, who is praised as Messiah within the Psalm. Through the centuries, the verse has been cherished as a prediction of the cross but was rejected as such by the Jews of the first two or three centuries. Thus, all crucifixes before the eleventh century portray Christ as robed and crowned.

But Jesus came as a King, and the throne from which He rules is not a gilded one as the thrones of earth, but the gory cross of Calvary. An old Latin hymn has it—

> Fulfilled is all that David told
> In true prophetic song of old;
> Amid the nations God, saith he,
> Hath reigned and triumphed from the tree.

The truth, then, we are setting out to state is that in the realm of grace, Christ reigns from His cross. As the Crucified One, His tree is His throne. The dying Savior was the triumphant Lord. He died not as a victim but as Victor.

> The truth that David learned to sing,
> Its deep fulfilment here attains:
> "Tell all the earth, the Lord is King!"
> Lo, from the cross, a King He reigns![21]

John Ellerton's lines suggest a similar thought—

> Throned upon the awful tree,
> King of grief, I watch with thee.

As Jesus died, His lips were opened seven times, and in His last utterances, we have a striking witness of His sovereignty. And it is not without significance that there are seven sayings, seeing that in such a sevenfold completeness, we have a revelation of the perfection of Christ's supremacy or sovereignty within the realm of grace.

The order or progress of the seven cries is also Christlike, for He began with His enemies and ended with Himself. All through His life, it was "others first, self last." Thus Jesus died even as He had lived.

---

21. Quoted in Philip Schaff, *Christ in Song*, vol. 1 (New York: Anson D. F. Randolph & Company, 1895), 160.

SOVEREIGN GRACE

The first thing Jesus did when He got to His cross was to seek forgiveness for those who had placed Him on it. He interceded for pardon for His enemies in virtue of His blood now freely flowing. There was forgiveness with Him that He might be feared.

What supreme magnanimity! How kingly and kind! What triumph it was when, in spite of agony of body as He died, He could yet realize the fatherhood of God and plead for the forgiveness of a fatherly heart!

In the morning of His life, even at the early age of twelve, His heart was warmed with the thought of a Father's love. And now, in the blackest hour of life, faith does not fail, for He is still able to say, *"Father"* (Luke 23:34).

Do we reign with Christ in the matter of forgiveness? Are we tenderhearted, forgiving one another even as God, for Christ's sake, forgave us? (See Ephesians 4:32.) What is our attitude when others wrong us? Our participation in the forgiveness of the cross demands that we forgive until seventy times *seven*. (See Matthew 18:21–22.)

SOVEREIGN POWER

"Today shalt thou be with me in paradise" (Luke 23:43). Such a part of the crucifixion story is like a flower of rare beauty planted among dreary crags of agony and blood. Robert Browning has reminded us that it was a thief who said the last kind word to Christ. At the very depth of His anguish, the malefactor recognized Jesus as a king about to possess a kingdom, and amid the mockery and scorn of men, he acclaimed His lordship. The others spurned His kingly claims, but this pardoned rebel craved a place in His kingdom.

And Christ poured an overflowing reward upon the dying thief who recognized His sovereignty. In the morning, the robber was out of Christ—at noon, in Christ—in the evening, with Christ. Guilt, grace, and glory, then, were the three stages in the spiritual biography of the thief on the cross.

Thus he became the first subject of the new kingdom of grace, the first sinner washed in the blood of the Lamb to enter paradise.

Christ was not too absorbed in His own agonies as to forget the dire spiritual need of a sin-stained fellow sufferer. Although His hand was nailed to the cross, He died as a King indeed, seeing that He had power to open the door of eternal bliss for a believing soul to enter with Himself.

And we likewise reign in life when the cross fills our vision, delivering us thereby from all self-centeredness. Are we endeavoring to make others the sharers of His bliss? Or do we hug to ourselves our knowledge of Christ and His salvation, forgetting the need of multitudes who do not know Him?

SOVEREIGN LOVE

Turning from the outer circles of sin-blinded Jews, brutal soldiers, and a callous thief, Jesus occupies Himself with those within the inner circle so dear to His loving heart. *"Woman, behold thy son!…Behold thy mother!"* (John 19:26–27). Here we find Christ reigning in thoughtfulness and consideration as He dies upon the tree. His noble mother and beloved disciple are in His thoughts amid final agonies. Tenderly He commends them to each other. What supremacy!

The hour of death has been called—

> That dark hour when bands remove,
> And none are named but names of love.[22]

Well, in His dying moments, Christ was concerned about the future welfare of her who had borne Him and whose soul was now pierced with a sword. Out of His deep poverty, He had already made precious gifts. To His murderers He bequeathed the forgiveness of His Father; to His companion in crucifixion the prospects and pleasures of paradise. Now His mother and His best-loved disciple, His two most coveted treasures on earth, He bequeaths to each other. He had no earthly possessions to leave His mother. Bringing nothing into the world with Him as He entered, He had nothing to will as He went out. He died as

22. Thomas Aird, "My Mother's Grave."

poor as He had lived. All that He could give was a son to His mother to fill His place, and a mother to His friend, who possibly was motherless and needed her care.

What a lesson there is in our Lord's loving consideration for others for this thoughtless, cruel, ungrateful age! We live in a heartless world. Thousands weep because of forgotten, unrewarded kindnesses. No matter what cross we have, let us determine to manifest the kingly grace of kindness to those who need and deserve it.

SOVEREIGN SACRIFICE

None will ever be able to plumb the depth of the awful words *"My God, my God, why hast thou forsaken me?"* (Matthew 27:46). Here we come to a more inner circle still, for in this cry, the Savior speaks to none but God. Around there was dense darkness, seeing that the Light of the World was being extinguished. Within the Savior's heart, however, there was blacker darkness, for His orphaned cry reveals a crucifixion of heart.

In such a dark moment, Jesus felt the terribleness of the load of human sin. Our weighty sins made His cross so heavy. But God, in His tenderness, drew the drapery of darkness around His beloved Son to hide His anguish from human gaze. At His birth, night became light; at His death, light became night.

But, blessed be His name, He stayed upon the cross. He endured that Godforsaken feeling in order that we might be forever saved. And now He reigns from the tree because of all He suffered thereon.

Is such a cross mine today? Have I the feeling of being Godforsaken? Has the sun's face been hidden, and does darkness cloud my life? Well, if I cannot trace God, I can yet trust Him. In moments of extreme anguish, Jesus could still say, *"My God, my God."* O to feel the pressure of His hand, even in the dark!

SOVEREIGN HUMILIATION

For twenty hours, the royal Sufferer had tasted nothing. For six hours, His beautiful yet battered body had hung upon the cross, and now that the tide of grief was assuaged, He was able to realize, in some measure, what He had endured. Vinegar was offered to Him, but He would not touch it. Possibly Satan plied Him with the old temptation "Command water to quench your thirsty lips." He refused, however, the opiate of man, and any effort of His own to slake a conscious thirst. Easily He could have refreshed Himself, but He went the limit in sacrifice.

> His are the thousand sparkling rills
> That from a thousand fountains burst,
> And fill with music all the hills;
> And yet he saith, "I thirst."[23]

What condescension! What kingly humiliation! The One of infinite fullness, who created all streams and wells, is now smitten with a bitter, burning, raging thirst. And truly, He was never as kingly as when, in His cry for water, He revealed His humanity. He humbled Himself! And, if we would resemble His kingliness, we must be prepared to travel with Him into the depths of humility. Joseph reached his throne with Pharaoh by the way of a dungeon. *"He that humbleth himself shall be exalted"* (Luke 14:11).

Christ's thirst, however, suggests a twofold thirst all of us must experience if we would reign in life. There is a thirst for God, for the accompaniment of the divine will, for the rest of faith, for deeper holiness of life. And then we must know something of that undying thirst for souls, for the rescue of those who sit at the world's broken cisterns, which can hold no water. And all who thirst in these directions shall be filled.

SOVEREIGN PROVISION

We have now reached the paean of victory—*"It is finished"* (John 19:30). What triumph! This acclamation is the cry of a Victor. Man is born to live; Christ was born to die. He was manifested that He might destroy the works of the devil. The cross, then, was the Savior's ruddy

---

23. Cecil F. Alexander, "His Are the Thousand Sparkling Rills."

throne upon which He stripped all hellish forces of their authority. Calvary was Satan's waterloo. No wonder the early fathers spoke of the cross as "the finished work of Christ."

God makes us more kingly in completion. Life, alas, is strewn with unfinished tasks; it is full of ragged edges. Like the man in the gospel story, we begin to build but are not able to finish. May grace be ours to accomplish the work heaven grants us to do!

SOVEREIGN TRUST

A voluntary committal and dismissal is implied in the cry *"Father, into thy hands I commend my spirit"* (Luke 23:46). Here Jesus gives up the ghost or dismisses His spirit. Willingly He stayed upon the bloody cross until He had drained the dregs of the bitter cup of suffering. He could have died sooner had He wished. His life, however, had been one of trust, and He now reigns in trust. "Trust in God is the last of all things, and the whole of all things," says Frederick William Faber. Thus Jesus died as He had lived, committing Himself to God.

And if, like Him, we, too, would reign in life and then in death, we must know how to commit our way unto the Lord. Our cross can become a throne only as we trust ourselves to God's fatherly care. Are you falling beneath your cross or are you reigning from it? Are you a conqueror in spite of your Calvary?

> Nailed to the racking cross, than bed of down
> More dear, whereon to stretch myself and sleep:
> So did I win a kingdom, share my crown;
> A harvest, come and reap.[24]

It is indeed a fearful thing to fall into the hands of a living God, to be dragged out of life with uncleansed sin on the soul. Better far to rest in His fatherly hands of grace and at death to go home to Him as Jesus did, as His life expired.

---

24. Christina G. Rossetti, "The Love of Christ Which Passeth Knowledge," *Goblin Market: And Other Poems* (London: Macmillan and Company, 1865), 133.

8

A CROSSLESS CHRIST

Throned upon the awful tree"[25] is how the death of Christ has been forcefully yet truthfully described. His crucifixion was His coronation; His cross was His crown, and He wears forever the insignia of royalty in the wound-prints admired by heaven's adoring host. His rich wounds still visible above remain as the evidence of redemption. Yet, although the cross is the wisdom of God, it is but foolishness in the eyes of man. Christ is wanted but not His cross. The two, however, are eternally nailed together.

The desire for a crossless Christ sprang from the religious people of His day, and it is still associated with the same quarter. Modern religion wants to retain a beautiful Jesus but not the blood-stained Man of Calvary. Christ is preached but not Christ crucified. The mangled, bleeding, dying form of the One who suffered for lost, guilty, hell-deserving sinners is the unwanted Christ of today. The blood must be expunged from theology and hymnology. A brutal cross is repugnant to the fine, cultured taste of man. Salvation by blood is treated as a "slaughterhouse" salvation and is a relic of the past. But the Bible would have us know that if there is no cross, there is no Christ; no atonement, no access; no death, no deliverance; no Golgotha, no glory; no blood, no blessing.

Mark's narrative of the crucifixion presents us with a faithful description of the treatment meted out to Christ and His cross.

25. John Ellerton, "Throned upon the Awful Tree," 1875.

FALSE HONOR

Not only were the chief priests heartlessly cruel in the death they gave Christ; spiritual mockery was also heaped upon Him by men who prided themselves on their religion. When they called him *"Christ the King of Israel"* (Mark 15:32), they ascribed honor to Him with mocking, hypocritical lips, for they made Him die like a felon on a wooden gibbet.

They named Him *Christ!* When He was named thus, He received His rightful title, for He was the Lord's Anointed. Eyes, however, blinded by tradition and prejudice, did not see Him as God's sent One. Flesh and blood can never have such a revelation. The divine estimate of the Son is given by the Father. (See Matthew 16:16–17.) Without the grace of the Spirit, Jesus can never be called "Lord."

They named Him *King of Israel!* Although born as such, tauntingly He is spoken of as the King for those for whom He came. A strange King, this. Yet this despised and rejected One dying like a criminal is God's appointed Ruler. At the zenith of Jesus' power, the Jews would have taken Him by force to make Him their King. The blood-bespattered Man of Calvary, however, was not their idea of a sovereign. They wanted a King on a throne in heaven, not on a tree of shame. And there are still those who want to take Jesus down from the cross and honor Him as Lord or Teacher; but, if His cross is belittled, such honor is false honor, no matter how reverently He is treated. There is no Christ but the Crucified One. Some there are who preach Christ, but there they stop. Paul, however, determined to know nothing among men save Christ and Him crucified.

DIABOLICAL TREATMENT

Men hate the cross because it reveals how low and base human nature is. It presents God at His best but man at his worst. It exhibits the greatest love on the part of heaven and the greatest hate on the part of earth. Surely it is absurd to speak about the good or the divine in man after his treatment of Christ on the cross.

1. SHAME AND SUFFERING

Jesus was classed by religious men as the vilest of the vile. *"With him they crucify two thieves"* (Mark 15:27). To His crucifiers, Christ was of no more value than robbers dying for their crimes. Where do you place Christ? Is it still between two thieves—sin within an evil heart and the world without and around? And yet even here there is the underlying thought of sovereignty, for He had the central place, even among thieves.

2. DERISION AND DEATH

What harsh and hellish treatment Jesus received by one and all! He was scorned, seeing that He was apparently helpless to save Himself, in spite of His claims to kingship. The passersby railed on Him—the priests mocked Him—the thieves reviled Him. And the cross is still gruesome to unbelief. The children of Christ's rejecters are with us today, for many revile and mock when a crucified Christ is presented. The cultured Greek of Paul's day despised the preaching of the cross. (See 1 Corinthians 1:21.) Yet it pleased God through the foolishness of such preaching to save those who believed. And Christ bleeding and dying on a cross to save a world of sinners lost and ruined by the fall may still appear to some minds as foolishness. Yet it remains as God's way of deliverance. Calvary is, indeed, an ugly, shameful scene, but it makes for beauty when its revelation is received and believed.

BLIND UNBELIEF

The command for Christ to descend from the cross indicated the crowd's desire for a display of miraculous power before they could accept His claims to be the Messiah. *"Descend now from the cross, that we may see and believe"* (Mark 15:32). Jesus, however, never performed miracles to satisfy idle curiosity. He believed in the economy of divine strength.

The world's axiom is, "Seeing is believing." Thus was it on the day Christ died. *"That we may see and believe."* They wanted to live by sight and not faith. But faith's attitude is the reverse: "Believing is seeing." Scripture says, *"Blessed are they that have not seen, and yet have believed"* (John 20:29). Jesus, of course, could have come down and demonstrated

His power, winning thereby the unbelievers who taunted Him. However, He voluntarily remained on the cross.

WHY CHRIST STAYED ON THE CROSS

Christ did not satisfy the craving for the spectacular. It was imperative for Him to stay on His cross for at least three reasons.

1. HE COULD NOT DISOBEY HIS FATHER

The cross was God's will for Christ, and He accepted it most gladly. *"I delight to do thy will, O my God"* (Psalm 40:8). Gethsemane had heard His prayer *"Nevertheless not my will, but thine, be done"* (Luke 22:42; see also Mark 14:36).

2. HE COULD NOT BREAK THE SCRIPTURES

Had Jesus complied with the rash request to descend from the cross, God's eternal truth would have been broken. In Daniel's day, it had been prophesied that the Messiah would be cut off. (See Daniel 9:26; Isaiah 53:10–12.) It was only by His death on the cross that Scripture was fulfilled. (See Psalm 22.)

3. HE COULD NOT SUFFER MAN TO PERISH

Love for man, and not mere Roman nails, kept Christ on His cross. He died that men might not perish. Knowing that without shedding of blood there could be no remission of sins, He gave His life as a ransom for many. (See Matthew 20:28; Mark 10:45.) Christ willingly took the crushing load of guilt upon His back.

UNWANTED CROSS

Come down from the cross! Why do men crave for religion without a Redeemer, for truth without the tree, for a Savior without sacrifice, for glory without a gibbet? We are living in days when even preachers are becoming all too silent regarding the necessity of proclaiming the blood as man's only hope. Let us examine one or two reasons why some people prefer a crossless Christ in these present evil days.

1. IT REVEALS THE HEART OF MAN

The cross exposes the sinner's guilt and unmasks his innate hatred for holiness. It likewise reveals man's hatred for Christ, God's ideal for man. At Calvary, we have the climax of sin, for man is seen at his worst. Convicted of sinfulness by the unsullied holiness of Jesus, man was eager to destroy Him.

2. IT DECLARES THE PURPOSE OF GOD

Calvary stands out as a tragic blunder if man can satisfy the claims of divine righteousness apart from the crimson stream. Christ came and died that the works of the devil might be destroyed; and the cross is God's only way of life and liberty. To be saved through blood-shedding may be humbling to the human heart; man, with his self-confidence and self-righteousness may reject the cross; but he cannot approach God by way of anything else. He is absolutely shut up to the mediatorial work of Jesus Christ. (See John 14:6.)

The cross, then, declares the need of a substitute, of atonement by blood as the only means of access. A man can be lost in very many ways, but he can be saved only in one way, namely, by the blood of Jesus Christ.

3. IT PRESENTS A PATTERN OF LIFE

To accept Christ involves the acceptance of a cross. As disciples, we must take up our cross and follow Jesus. Alas, some are willing to be religious but unwilling to die to the world and to their own way. They want a Christ without a cross. In their heart of hearts, they know what God desires of them; but the divine voice is smothered. Conscience is unwilling to pay the price of a thoroughly saved life.

But as we require a Christ on His cross to save us and to satisfy the claims of God on our behalf, and as Christ and His cross are eternally one and He still bears the marks of anguish, we, too, as Christians must experience co-crucifixion. (See Galatians 6:14.)

There is no such person as a crossless Christian, even as there is no crossless Christ. Believing in the crucified Christ, we must live the crucified life. The scars of separation from sin and the world must be evident. Yes, and the more real our identification with the cross, the deeper the hatred of those around us. If, like Simon, we bear His cross, we shall quickly discover that it has lost none of its shame and contempt.

And, further, if we would reign in life, we must reign from a cross. Life comes as we die to the allurements of the world, the flesh, and the devil. So Jesus offers you what your sin gave Him, namely, a cross. Will you accept it? Are you so captivated by His cross as to surrender all the vain things that charm you most? Friends may ostracize you as your separation becomes more evident, but you must stay on your cross for Him, just as He stayed on His cross for you.

Lord Jesus, by Thy wounded feet, O guide my feet aright;
Lord Jesus, by Thy wounded hands, O keep my hands from wrong;
Lord Jesus, by Thy parched lips, O curb my cruel tongue;
Lord Jesus, by Thy closed eyes, O guard my wayward sight;
Lord Jesus, by Thy thorn-crowned brow, O purify my mind;
Lord Jesus, by Thy pierced heart, O knit my heart to Thine!

9

MYSTICAL TRANSFUSION

"The life of the flesh is in the blood."
—Leviticus 17:11

The transfusion of blood from one person to another is a wonderful discovery of science, whereby the fresh life of a healthy body is imparted to a dying person in order to restore expiring life. The weak, diseased, impoverished blood of a sufferer is vivified and strengthened by the impartation of the pure, vigorous blood of one with a sound body. And there are many blood donors who are willing to pour their life-stream into a reserve for use in critical cases.

THE EFFICACY OF THE BLOOD OF JESUS

Years ago, I witnessed a noble sacrifice of blood. A friend of mine saw his wife languishing on a bed of pain. Gradually she grew worse, necessitating an immediate and serious operation. After such she seemed to be slipping through the fingers of the surgeons who battled for her life. A blood transfusion was the last resort, and the devoted, anxious husband, taking a bed in a neighboring ward of the hospital, gave his precious blood, again and again, until fresh vigor shot through the weak frame of the woman he loved. And such an incident and fact of surgical science suggests one or two helpful spiritual parallels as we come to think about the efficacy of the blood of Jesus.

THE NEED OF THE SUFFERER

There was that dear woman in a weak, dying condition, with exhausted life-germs and unable to resist the death-germs battling for supremacy. What a picture this is of the sinner who is weak and helpless and ready to die! Unless help reaches him from an outside source, he will perish in his sins, for he is without strength to save himself.

THE SACRIFICE OF THE FRIEND

That loving husband could not bear to see his wife suffer. She needed fresh blood, and so he allowed his own veins to be ripped open, that healthy blood might be pumped into the wasted form of the sufferer. Thus he gave part of himself to save his wife, for the life of the flesh is in the blood. And the blood Christ shed for our redemption was the blood of a Friend and the Lover of our souls.

It is clearly evident, of course, that all blood-tapping is not successful. If transfusion is to be effective, the blood given and imparted must be pure, untainted by disease, and possessed of strong, active cells. There is the secret of Christ's efficacious blood shed upon the shameful tree for our sins—it was so pure, holy, warm, and powerful. It was the blood of God's beloved Son.

THE NATURE OF THE BLOOD

John's rich statement about the blood of Jesus Christ, God's Son, having power to cleanse from all sin, has become so commonplace that its deep significance is somehow lost upon us.

THE *BLOOD*

Blood is the symbol of life. The difference between a corpse and a live person is that one has living blood coursing through his veins and the other does not. And outpoured blood is a symbol of life given. The blood Jesus spilt at the cross, then, signified the outpouring of His life. He had power to lay down His life, and willingly He sacrificed it, that we might live. And now, when we speak and sing about being washed in the blood of the Lamb, we do not mean that the blood as a possession still exists but that, in virtue of Calvary, God can receive the sinner. The blood represents the abiding efficacy of the cross; and if only those who find the preaching and teaching about the blood repugnant would remember such a fact they would come to value the finished work of Calvary in a new way.

THE BLOOD OF *JESUS*

Jesus, the human One. Surely this thought has a tender appeal. The blood of Jesus was rich, warm, human blood. It was the blood of One who was so kind, sympathetic, and compassionate. It was blood outpoured for friend and foe alike. Jesus said, *"My blood...is shed for you"* (Luke 22:20). What an offering to make that unworthy sinners might be saved!

THE BLOOD OF JESUS *CHRIST*

Christ, the Anointed One! So the blood was not only real, human blood but royal blood—the blood of the Messiah, a *King*. We talk about those of Royal House as being of royal blood. Well, Christ has royal blood, seeing that He was the eternal King. Thus when He died, He shed blood not of a poor, despised Jew or Nazarene, but of the Sent One of God. And if "there is power where the word of a king is" (see Ecclesiastes 8:4), what great power the blood of the King of Kings must have!

THE BLOOD OF JESUS CHRIST, *HIS SON*

His Son! So the bloodshed was the blood of the divine One. And it is this fact that adds efficacy to the blood. Had it been the blood of an ordinary man, it would never have availed for men. But there is power in Christ's shed blood in that it was the blood of God. (See Acts 20:28.) The blood of the God-man! Yes, but here we enter a mystery too deep and profound for words. The great miracle of the virgin birth was the fusion of deity and humanity, the welding of godhead and manhood into one personality. Thus, when Jesus died, He shed the blood of the God-man created by the Holy Spirit within the womb of Mary. This, then, is the reason why the blood can cleanse from all sin and why Satan strives to thwart the preaching of the cross.

"The blood of Jesus Christ his Son cleanseth us from all sin" (1 John 1:7)! Cleanses from *all* sin. Yes, from all kinds and acts of sin!

CHARACTERISTICS OF THE BLOOD

O the countless victories of the blood! May we never tire of exalting its glorious triumphs! The blood, as we have seen, represents the finished work of Christ at Calvary for sinners everywhere, and John sings of three glorious virtues of the blood of God's dear Son.

These are the three notes in this blood-glorifying song:

1. IT HAS PERPETUAL CLEANSING

In 1 John 1:7, the word *"cleanseth"* is in the present tense, implying that the blood keeps on cleansing. Its efficacy is continuous; it never loses its power to save and deliver. Age after age, it retains its capacity of cleansing. The crimson stream never ceases, at any moment, to function as a channel of pardon. In the hour of our salvation, we experienced deliverance from the guilt of sin as the Spirit applied the blood to our hearts; but every hour of every day since the happy day that fixed our choice on Christ, the healing virtue of the blood has been pleaded on our behalf. Each moment, we require its washing and loosing power. (See Revelation 1:5.)

> Dear dying Lamb, Thy precious blood
> Shall never lose its power,
> Till all the ransomed Church of God
> Be saved, to sin no more.[26]

2. IT HAS PERSONAL CLEANSING

Whatever our need may be, each of us can lay his finger on this verse and claim it as his own. Martin Luther has told us to watch the pronouns of Scripture. And here is one to appropriate. May we learn how to translate *"us"* into *"me"*!

John, of course, is writing to saints; thus, his message about the cleansing blood has a direct application to believers, all of whom need a daily washing from the defilement of sin. The apostle has in mind the practice of sin rather than its principle—fruit rather than root—sins

---

26. William Cowper, "There Is a Fountain Filled with Blood," 1772.

rather than sin. And the blood of Jesus Christ keeps on cleansing us from our association with sin as we endeavor to abide in unbroken fellowship with God.

3. IT HAS PERFECT CLEANSING

John declares that the blood of God's Son is able to cleanse from all sin. It is a tremendous but a blessedly true fact. And all means *all!* Secret sins, presumptuous sins, sins of youth and age, sins against others, sins against ourselves, darker sins against God. Yes, the blood can deal with all kinds and degrees of sin because of its royal, rich nature. Shed over 1900 years ago, its abiding efficacy is experienced the moment a conscious-stricken sinner turns to the Savior. Immediately the miracle happens—the red blood of Jesus makes the black heart white as snow. (See Isaiah 1:18.)

THE ACT OF TRANSFUSION

We can glean another truth from the blood transfusion incident told at the beginning of this chapter. There came the exact moment when the blood of the husband was drained and conveyed to the body of his suffering wife. The Holy Spirit is the great Transfuser, the divine Surgeon who, with wondrous skill, causes the virtue and efficacy of the cross to pass into sinful, needy lives. It is He who applies the blood to the sinner as he turns to the Savior. And well might each of us pray, "O blessed Surgeon, transfuse more of the precious, priceless, powerful blood of Jesus into my poor, weak life, that life more abundant may be mine."

In his monumental study of Genetic Theology, Dr. John B. Champion relates the story of a somewhat fastidious lady who always objected to both Scripture lessons and hymns mentioning the blood. When such a hymn as "There Is a Fountain Filled with Blood" was sung, she was so disturbed that she would leave the worship service.

This went on for some time, until she contracted an anemic condition. The time came when but one thing could save her life—a blood transfusion. While several persons, including her husband, volunteered to give their blood, her husband's proved best suited to hers. After the transfusion, which had restored her health, her attitude completely changed. Her life was saved at the cost of a blood transfusion, a sacrifice on her husband's part, and the blood became a saving, sacred, divine thing to her. From her experience, she could understand how Christ's saving life had entered into her own and how His sacrificial life had redeemed her.

After this, she could not hear too much about the redeeming blood of Christ. Hymns telling of the "sacrifice of nobler name and richer blood" than "all the blood…on Jewish altars slain"[27] was now a heavenly melody in her ears. Experience had lifted her up to the language of the blood.

Some professing to be refined may scoff at the gospel of blood and call it a slaughterhouse salvation. They forget, however, that animals slain in a slaughterhouse are killed that they might have physical life. Man may reject the blood of Christ, but without it, he is hopelessly lost, *"for it is the blood that maketh an atonement for the soul"* (Leviticus 17:11).

---

27. Isaac Watts, "Not All the Blood of Beasts," 1709.

10

LEST WE FORGET

"This do in remembrance of me."
—Luke 22:19

*"The Holy Ghost, whom the Father will send in my name,
he shall...bring all things to your remembrance."*
—John 14:26

The combination of these two sentences in our Lord's teaching indicates the two sides of the remembrance involved in the sacramental feast He Himself instituted. There is a human side—*"This do."* This command is fulfilled when we come together in obedience to the express will of the Master. But, knowing the weakness of our memory, God urges us to sit at His Table as often as we can to remember His dying love.

Then there is the divine side—*"The Holy Ghost...shall...bring all things to your remembrance."* Happily we are not left to our own effort to stimulate remembrance. It is the function of the Spirit to quicken our memories and take us back to the cross. We are sluggish, forgetful, and need to be constantly reminded by One who witnessed the tragedy of Calvary. Thus, the Wind of Pentecost keeps alive the fire of Calvary. The Holy Spirit keeps the cross before our eyes. And He delights to carry our minds back to the victory of Calvary, which made possible His descent at Pentecost.

As we gather round the Table of the Lord, the Spirit constantly reminds us of three realms of truth and quickens our faith in such. He presents God in His love, justice, and holiness; He proclaims Christ in His sacrifice and humiliation; and He manifests man in his sin, need, and impotence. And how we should praise the Spirit for His goodness in stirring up our minds by way of remembrance!

In one of his incomparable devotional volumes, Dr. J. R. Miller tells the story of a dear mother who lost her only child. What grief was hers! Now and again, she would go to the drawer and, taking out the toys, shoes, and garments of the departed baby, fondly handle them. Such articles inspired remembrance, and remembrance produced many qualities. Let us take a look at a few.

REMEMBRANCE QUICKENS LOVE

The love of that mother for her child was quickened or intensified by remembrance. That mother did not bury her love in a grave. Love is of God and is therefore eternal. Love will last as long as God.

It is thus that the Holy Spirit seeks to stimulate a purer, deeper love for Jesus in us. He takes us back to the cross, where we seem to hear the Savior ask, *"Lovest thou me?"* (John 21:17). And as we remember the cost of our salvation, what reply do we have but, "I love Thee for wearing the thorns on Thy brow."[28] We hear a good deal about a passion for souls, but our tragedy is that we do not have enough passion for Jesus Himself. Count Zinzendorf's confession was, "I have but one passion: It is He, it is He alone." Do we love Him, seeing that He first loved us? (See 1 John 4:19.)

One difference, however, between the fond mother Dr. Miller writes about and ourselves is this—the mother had seen the face of her child, looked into his eyes, kissed his cheeks, and hugged him to her breast. But we have never seen the face of Christ. Our eyes have never seen that radiant form of His. The Holy Spirit, however, makes Him real to us through faith. *"Whom having not seen, ye love"* (1 Peter 1:8; see also John 20:29).

---

28. William Ralph Featherstone, "My Jesus, I Love Thee."

> Yet, though I have not seen, and still
> Must rest in faith alone,
> I love Thee, dearest Lord, and will,
> Unseen, but not unknown.

REMEMBRANCE BEGETS GRATITUDE

As that lonely hearted mother handled her baby's possessions, surely she would raise gratitude to God for the life given even though his stay was so short. She would say to herself, "Well, "Tis better to have loved and lost than never to have loved at all.'"[29] She would be grateful that her child died young and innocent, being spared the sin and shame of life. Her son gathered home to God's pure lilies, the mother would come to know that, after all, there are worse experiences than that of having a child in heaven.

It is thus that the Spirit works. He makes real the debt of gratitude we owe. The purpose of the Lord's Table each time we sit to eat and drink is that we might say with deeper feeling, "Thank you, Lord, for bearing my curse and dying my death." Why, Christ Himself gave thanks as He broke the bread He said would symbolize His broken body. Gave thanks! What was He thankful for? Was it not for the assurance that by His death a mighty deliverance would be wrought for multitudes of captive souls?

REMEMBRANCE FOSTERS HOLINESS

Faith would assure the mother that her dear child is in heaven, made holy and dressed in white forever. And such contemplation would inspire her to face life with a more earnest endeavor to correspond in some measure to the purity of her child above.

A great question troubling many hearts is whether our departed loved ones are cognizant of what goes on below; whether they can see and know all things of human interest. Well, if they share the omniscience of the Lord, into whose likeness they have been transformed,

---

29. Alfred Lord Tennyson, *In Memoriam A. H. H,* 1849.

then they do not sorrow as those of earth, for like their Lord, they, too, can see the end from the beginning.

While, of course, our holy dead can have no contact with us, is it yet not a spur to holy living to realize that kindred spirits are not very far away and that possibly they carry a definite interest in our lives? This we know, the remembrance of the crucified, risen, exalted yet absent Lord leads us to a more complete surrender. As we remember that His grief and pains were involved in our redemption, what else can we do but be holy and live fully surrendered to Him?

There may be some uncertainty regarding the knowledge our departed have of earth or of how near they are to us, but of this we are certain, that Jesus is ever near. We feel and know that He is at hand. And the more conscious we are of His presence, the deeper our consciousness of sin, and the more determined our desire is to live as unto Him.

> I see Thee not, I hear Thee not,
> Yet art Thou oft with me;
> And earth hath ne'er so dear a spot
> As where I meet with Thee.[30]

REMEMBRANCE INSPIRES ANTICIPATION

Let us turn again to the fond mother we have been considering. The house is quiet and memory is active. Going to the drawer yet once again, she handles those precious shoes and little garments, and sits and thinks of the love she bore and still bears for the innocent child. How grateful to God she is for the joy of motherhood even though it was short-lived. Rising from her reveries, she goes on her journey inspired to holier living, realizing that the separation is but for a little. Before long, she will clasp him again, and death will never more tear him from her heart! With half of her heart in heaven, she brushes aside her tears and is cheered by the thought of a blissful reunion.

---

30. Ray Palmer.

It is thus that the Holy Spirit works. In His effort to quicken our remembrance, He bids us look back to the grave where Jesus lay—up to His present abode—forward to the day when we shall see Him face-to-face. As the mother is saved from nursing her grief by remembering the future, and gathers hope for her bruised heart thereby, so the Holy Spirit inspires anticipation. As we take the bread and the wine in our hands, He reminds us that such remembrance is only *"till he come"* (1 Corinthians 11:26).

Atonement and advent are seen to be two halves of one whole. And what a gathering of the ransomed that will be! "And with the morn those angel faces smile."[31] His face, however, will be the one all the redeemed will adore. The mother went out to meet her beloved child, to be joined with him forever; but Christ is coming out to meet us. And what a blessed meeting that will be! Such blessed anticipation, as well as love, gratitude, and holiness, is fostered by the remembrance feast.

Dr. J. R. Miller also tells the story of a young man who went abroad. Before setting out, he was presented with a watch having upon its dial miniatures of his loving parents.

"Take this watch," said his father, "and carry it with you in all your journeyings. Every time you look to see the hour—the eyes of your father and mother will look into yours. When you see these home faces, remember that we are thinking of you and praying for you. Go to no place...where you would not want us to see you. Do nothing that you would not want us to witness."

Jesus has given us His own picture in the Lord's Supper, so to speak. His broken body and shed blood are ever before us as we participate in it. And as we look at the dial bearing His portrait, we are saved from doubt, fear, and sin. Remembrance intensified by the Spirit leads us to greater nobleness and beauty of life. And, living in the light of His return, we have the assurance that when He summons us, we shall pass out to meet our Beloved without the blush of shame.

---

31. John Henry Newman, "The Pillar of Cloud."

11

THE MAGNETISM OF CALVARY

"And I, if I be lifted up from the earth,
will draw all men unto me."
—John 12:32

There are at least two thoughts within the narrative leading up to the unique verse before us, describing as it does the magnetism of the cross.

First is the Greek's request—*"Sir, we would see Jesus"* (John 12:21). One cannot say what it was that actually drew these Gentiles to Christ. Perhaps it was curiosity, which is often the mother of wonder, or the minister of deathless devotion, as it was in the experience of Zacchaeus. Or possibly heart hunger compelled the searchers to seek out Jesus. Grecian art, music, and philosophy supplied no bread for their dissatisfied souls; thus they found their way to Him who came as the Bread of Life. If the latter is true, that unsatisfied craving and unrest of soul brought these Greeks to Jesus, then in such we have a foreshadowing of the participation of the great Gentile world in the redemptive work of the cross.

Second is the Master's response—*"Except a corn of wheat fall into the ground and die"* (John 12:24). If these Greeks' love for the beautiful led them to the beautiful One, then they must learn that Jesus cannot be known after the flesh. Only if He is known as the Crucified One can He be received and admired. And as a result of Calvary, He can draw both Jew and Gentile unto Himself. As the corn of wheat, He fell into the ground and died, but what a rich and plentiful harvest is His because of His death and resurrection.

HIS MAGNETIC PERSON

"I, if I" (John 12:32)! As such personal pronouns suggest His adorable Person, let us think, in the first place, of the Christ of the cross. Christ Himself is the most magnetic of all forces. *"Draw me, we will run after thee"* (Song of Solomon 1:4).

It is profitable to note the recurring *"I"* in our Lord's teaching. Here the pronoun is emphatic, "I and I" alone. What a stupendous claim to make! But as the Great I Am, He could make it without assumption. Repulsive in others, Christ's use of "I" is quite natural. Our constant usage of "I" savors of egotism. With Him, however, it is different. When this phrase left His lips, it carried divine authority. He could say and do all that He uttered and accomplished because of who and what He was. Deity is wrapped up in the pronoun.

Further, the "I" is used in opposition to *"the prince of this world"* (John 12:31). What a contrast of character! The Light of the World—the prince of the world. The one draws to life, the other to death. Jesus draws us to Himself with the cords of love—Satan draws us to himself with deceit and crafty subtlety.

HIS MAGNETIC PASSION

"Lifted up from the earth" (John 12:32)! So, from His person, we are led to His passion; from His deity, to His death; from His character, to His cross, from the Christ *of* the cross, to the Christ *on* the cross.

Three times the phrase *"lifted up"* is employed by Jesus in John's gospel, and each reference carries with it a different aspect of Calvary. For example, there is…

1. The reason for the cross. *"Even so must the Son of man be lifted up"* (John 3:14). Here we have the basis of regeneration. There can be no salvation without sacrifice.

2. The revelation of the cross. *"When ye have lifted up the Son of man, then shall ye know that I am he"* (John 8:28). Even the dying thief came to know that the dying One near to him was the Son of God with power to save. (See Luke 23:40–42.)

3. The reign of the cross. *"I, if I be lifted up from the earth, will draw all men unto me"* (John 12:32). And the cross is still the greatest "draw." Thus, the prophecy of Scripture—the ministry of the Holy Spirit and the perpetual ministry and power of the Crucified One—are happily blended.

The twofold aspect of Calvary is emphasized in the narrative we are considering. First of all, there is the *fact* of Christ's death, and then its *form*. The fact—the *"death he should die"* (John 18:32) indicates that the shadow was ever before Him. Man is born to live—Christ was born to die. He was virtually slain before He left the glory. The *form* of His death is implied in the phrase *"lifted up"* (John 12:32). Crucifixion was the Roman form of death meted out to malefactors, and your Lord and mine was treated as a felon when cruel hands nailed Him to a wooden gibbet. He was lifted up on the earth at His death, lifted out of the earth at His resurrection. Lifted up from the earth altogether at His ascension. And it takes all that is wrapped up in Christ's death, resurrection, and ascension to complete His drawing power. He died, He lives—this constitutes the saving gospel.

HIS MAGNETIC POWER

"I...will draw all men unto me." (John 12:32). *"A threefold cord is not quickly broken"* (Ecclesiastes 4:12). Thus we have our Lord's person, passion, and power. His deity, death, and dynamic, or the death of deified humanity, are all alike implied in Christ's declaration. So we have the Christ of the cross—*"I, if I"* (John 12:32); the Christ on the cross—*"Lifted up"* (verse 32); and the Christ through the cross—*"Draw all men unto me"* (verse 32). And, truly, there is no other way by which we can reach Him.

A gifted writer has pointed out that the magnetism of Christ is seen in that He lifts men up and unites them to God by *revelation*, by the gift of the Spirit of divine light, whereby the reign of night is ended; unites them to God by *redemption*, by the gift of divine life, whereby the reign of death is ended; and unites them to God by *inspiration*, by the gift of divine liberty, whereby the reign of infirmity is ended.

Several precious truths can be gleaned from this record of Christ's magnetic Calvary power. For example...

1. THE UPLIFTED LORD IS THE ONLY MAGNETIC POWER

No other truth can awaken men to a life of surrender and of devotion like that of the cross. They realize that love so amazing demands the very best they have to give. Yes, and the preaching of Christ crucified breaks up the frozen indifference of some hearts, and delivers them from inertia. The cross disturbs the conscience, awakens moral pains, accomplishes a spiritual resurrection, and draws souls to a life of undying love.

Sacrifice is always strangely magnetic. In common life, it never fails to allure one's interest and admiration. Some time ago in the "In Memoriam" column of a daily paper, the following notice occurred—"In memory of a lovely little lady, who made the supreme sacrifice of motherhood, leaving sweet memories but a brokenhearted hubby." Yet somehow the vast majority is unresponsive to the most supreme sacrifice of all. They can hear and read about the sufferings of Christ but be untouched and unmoved. A trashy novel can move them to tears, but to their cold, dead hearts, Calvary with all its horror and anguish has no appeal.

Further, if Christ is proclaimed as an ethical Teacher, such an aspect may arrest the mind, but it will never generate heat in a cold heart. If He is presented as a fiery Reformer, signatures may be gained from those who are willing to join in a crusade against glaring sins. As the young Prophet, He may draw the cheap, blind worship and mental assent of those who are out for hero-worship. If exalted as the lowly Galilean Peasant, He may draw the sympathy of humble souls who never reach higher than human feelings.

If, however, Christ is to deliver men from the penalty and pollution of sin, then He must be lifted up as the sacrificial Savior. As a beautiful Teacher, ardent Reformer, zealous Prophet, He may win the plaudits of men, but as the Son of God, crucified for sinners, He captivates souls and moves men to holier living and consecrated endeavor. Therefore let us make much of the cross, seeing that it has been the theme of all those who have been used of God. Persuaded that their only magnet was the Lord Jesus in the wonderful energies of His transcendent sacrifices and not in His beautiful teachings and incomparably lovely life, they lived to extol Him who died upon a rude and rugged gibbet.

2. BEING ABOVE, HE CAN DRAW FROM BENEATH

Lifted up from the earth, Christ can draw men out of it!

The Christ some men preach can never draw, for they keep Him on the earth. They declare that He was only a man and no higher than others. He is relegated to the level of ordinary humanity, and such a perverted gospel has no magnetism whatever. Had He remained on the earth, power to save would never have been His. Crucified, however, He can conquer. A church or a Christian living on the level of the world can never draw souls nearer the Savior. Like Him, we must be raised from the earth if we would lift it up to God. Let us, therefore, exalt the cross both by lip and life.

3. THE UPLIFTED CHRIST POSSESSES A UNIVERSAL MAGNETISM

The cross draws *all* men. Truly this foreshadows the universality of the gospel with all nations, clans, conditions, participating in the fruits of Calvary.

But some heart may argue thus—"If Christ has power to draw all men, why are not all men saved?" Well, it is evident that the cross has sufficient efficacy to save all men. Universal attraction is focused in the sacrificial energy of His death—"The last fragrant syllable of God's utterance of love." Freedom of will and moral power, however, can resist the charm of the cross. It will be noticed that Christ "draws" not "drags." He strives to win souls, not worry souls. But His overtures can be rejected. "I would…you would not." (See Matthew 23:37.)

Thus the drawing and the coming are united. The magnet says "come" but "draws" as it speaks. (See Matthew 11:28; John 12:32.) Can your heart sing—

He drew me and I followed on,
Charmed to confess the voice divine.[32]

And, blessed be His name, the day is fast coming when the Master will appear in the air and, as a Magnet, draw all the blood-sheltered ones up to Himself. They will rise to Him as filings to a magnet.

4. THE MAGNETIC POWER OF CHRIST IS CONCENTRIC

If a standard was placed in the center of a building and people urged to get as near to it as possible, what would happen? Why, the nearer they found themselves to the standard, the nearer they would be to one another. And the nearer we live to the cross, the more we find ourselves drawn together. But somehow we have forgotten the Center. The church has created centers of her own, and if men do not travel to her center, there is judgment and expulsion.

Christianity, which ought to be the expression of brotherly love, has become the avenue of strife and isolation. Journeying from the cross, so-called Christians have separated from one another. And, whenever we plant our feet upon a self-chosen, self-created center, fighting only for a particular interpretation of a creed, and forgetting to keep our eyes fixed upon the uplifting Lord, we miss the superlative sacrifice of His cross. A return to the Crucified One would quickly heal the church's lamentable division.

5. THE MAGNETIC POWER OF THE CROSS IS CHRIST-O-CENTRIC

Christ on the cross is the center and circumference of all things. As the Crucified One, He draws all men unto Himself. He will not give His glory unto another. (See Isaiah 42:8.) There is a modern tendency to bring men to His works, His words, and His ways, rather than to Himself. And it is sadly possible to draw men to a church and yet not to Christ! Nothing, however, must obscure His adorable Person. Our ultimate goal must ever be to attract souls to the Master Himself.

May it ever be our passion to present the Savior in all the fullness of His grace and charm, that, seeing Him, hearts will be lost in the

32. Philip Doddridge, "O Happy Day, That Fixed My Choice," 1755.

contemplation of His majesty! Because He has power to lift men out of the cold prison-house of guilt, delivering them thereby from the bitterness of a Christ-less death, with its awful doom of abiding wrath, let us extol His virtue.

Martyrs, like Stephen, were forced into death. Christ, however, walked deliberately to His bitter end. He descended the slope of sacrifice from grade to grade until He tore out death's sting; and in one supreme victory, he triumphed over sin, death, and hell. Hallelujah, what a Savior![33]

The question is, have you allowed the uplifted Christ to draw you? May you sing,

> Drawn to the cross which Thou hast blessed
> With healing gifts for souls distressed,
> To find in Thee my life, my Rest,
> Christ crucified, I come!
>
> …
>
> To be what Thou wouldst have me be,
> Accepted, sanctified in Thee,
> Through what Thy grace shall work in me,
> Christ crucified, I come![34]

We read of those who came to Him from every quarter. If you know Him not, may you come to Him out of your need. May God enable you to yield to the charm of the cross!

---

33. Philip P. Bliss, 1875.
34. Genevieve Mary Irons, "Drawn to the Cross," 1881.

12

THE AFTERGLOW OF CALVARY

"Jesus himself drew near, and went with them."
—Luke 24:15

One never tires of reading that incomparable narrative of one ever memorable journey to Emmaus. It yields something fresh every time we turn to it. Trusting, loving, worshipping hearts love it because its revelation of the risen Lord as a Companion whose friendship is so real.

THE "OPENINGS" IN LUKE 24

As a whole, the chapter is unique in that it contains a series of "openings," seven of which can be traced.

AN OPENED GRAVE (SEE LUKE 24:2–3.)

How we praise the Lord that He did not remain in the grave! Every Lord's Day proclaims the fact of His glorious resurrection. Yes, and His empty tomb is likewise the pledge that the graves of His own will be emptied some day.

AN OPENED HOME (SEE LUKE 24:29.)

There was a home willing to entertain Him. May we ever be willing and ready to welcome Jesus into our heart, home, and life! Once admitted, He abides forevermore.

AN OPENED EYE (SEE LUKE 24:31.)

As then, so now we can only know Him as our eyes are opened by the Holy Spirit. Without Him, we can discern no beauty in Jesus. The Spirit is the anointing our eyes need to see in Christ, the fairest of all.

AN OPENED BIBLE (SEE LUKE 24:32.)

The mystic Book never yields its treasures to mere natural reason. God's Spirit alone can break the seals thereof. It is He who opens the Scriptures. As the divine Author of such, it is His prerogative to lead and guide us into truth.

AN OPENED MIND (SEE LUKE 24:45.)

For opened Scriptures, there must be an opened understanding. Eyes must be opened before they can behold wondrous things out of God's law. Alas! we are so dull, so slow to learn. Ignorance, prejudice, superstition, and tradition make it difficult for us to see.

AN OPENED HEAVEN (SEE LUKE 24:51.)

A door was opened in heaven allowing Jesus to return to His Father, and through the same opened heaven, the Holy Spirit came (see verse 49) as the gift of the ascended Lord to His believing people.

AN OPENED MOUTH (LUKE 24:53.)

The Old Testament prayer "O Lord, *open thou my lips; and my mouth shall shew forth thy praise*" (Psalm 51:15) is here answered. And what else could the disciples do but praise and bless God for the realization of the presence of a risen, glorified Lord?

THE EMMAUS JOURNEY

Coming to the actual Emmaus journey, there are several suggested truths for our hearts to ponder. The highway, alive with pedestrians and traffic coming and going, presented a busy scene. A sad pair, buried in their grief, trudged the thronged highway all unconscious of the jostling crowds. All at once, a Stranger joined them; and although they were unaware of the identity of this Companion, they were glad of someone to whom they could unbosom themselves. So Jesus went with them. Out on the highway? Yes, on the highway, for He is for the open places as well as for the quiet, secret solitudes.

1. THE PERSON ALL SUBLIME—"JESUS HIMSELF"

One peculiar feature of the New Testament is the emphasis it lays upon the person and not merely the power and possessions of the Savior. Jesus Himself dominates its pages. And we feel embarrassed when we come to handle the riches of His person. To try and fathom all that He is in Himself is like sailing on a shoreless ocean. Truly He is greater and grander than all His works. Christianity is a mass of marvels, but Christ is the greatest miracle—the Wonder of wonders. We praise Him for His Book, His day, His church, and His people; but He Himself has the place of preeminence. All that we have from Him are but broken lights of His perfect self. Our living, loving, lasting union is with Jesus Himself. C. H. Spurgeon has so beautifully expressed it, "Give me not his garments, though I prize every thread, but the blessed wearer whose sacred energy made even the hem thereof to heal with a touch." O may nothing obscure His person! Jesus Himself is the greatest delight of all.

Jesus Himself Is the Theme of Scripture

That day on the Emmaus road, Jesus poured the healing balm of His holy Word into the aching hearts of two disciples. (See Luke 24:27.) And light dawned upon their perplexed minds as they came to see the vital connection between the Scriptures and the Savior. *"In the volume of the book it is written of me"* (Psalm 40:7; Hebrews 10:7). And the Bible is only effectual as we see Jesus as the center and circumference of its contents. It ever gives zest to study when we look for Him in all we read.

Beyond the sacred page I seek Thee, Lord.[35]

---

35. Mary A. Lathbury, "Break Thou the Bread of Life," 1877.

Jesus Himself Is the Sacrifice for Sin

Jesus surrendered not merely His crown, His throne, and His heavenly joys, He gave Himself! With His own blood, He bought us. Job was stripped of much, but a limit was set upon what Satan could take. *"Only upon himself put not forth thine hand"* (Job 1:12). Jesus, however, knew no such limit. He saved others; Himself He did not save. (See Matthew 27:42.)

Jesus Himself Is the Companion of Life

Yes, we have the ministry of angels, and we owe more to them than we realize. And we have the gracious assistance of the Holy Spirit as we journey homeward. Saints also are often comforters and good companions. But we have Jesus all to ourselves, and He is better than the best. He will never leave us. (See Hebrews 13:5.)

Jesus Himself Is the Cure for Fearfulness

He is our Peace! Peace is the Person Himself. Out upon the storm-tossed sea of life, how calm we become when we hear His assuring voice say, *"It is I; be not afraid"* (Matthew 14:27; Mark 6:50; John 6:20). Trouble always ceases when we believe in Jesus. (See John 14:1.)

Jesus Himself Is Our Hope

He is not going to send an angel for us. *"The Lord himself shall descend from heaven"* (1 Thessalonians 4:16). And it is the personal return of our Lord, all advent Scripture affirms. (See John 14:3; Acts 1:10–11.)

Jesus Himself Desires Us All to Himself

Having made all things for Himself (see Proverbs 16:4), His heart is never satisfied unless He has us all to Himself. And He is jealous over us with a godly jealousy. (See Deuteronomy 4:24.) He will brook no rival. And, truly, He has every claim to all that we are and have.

There are some who crave this experience and the other. Highly emotional souls yearn for ecstatic feelings and thoughts. Jesus, however, has promised us not experiences but Himself. And holiness is simply the willingness to let Jesus appropriate more of the life day by day. May we become more occupied with Christ! Let us overcome Satan as he strives to keep us from the person of our blessed Lord.

> My goal is God Himself, not joy, nor peace,
> Nor even blessing, but Himself, my God;
> 'Tis His to lead me there—not mine, but His—
> At any cost, dear Lord, by any road.[36]

2. THE PRESENCE ALL GLORIOUS— "DREW NEAR"

The Lord in His person is wonderful and all-sublime, yet it is not less wonderful to realize that He has offered to grace our lives with His presence. Then, He is not only *dear* but *near*. With Israel, we, too, are a people near unto the Lord.

And such nearness is mutual; it operates from the divine and human sides. *"Draw nigh to God, and he will draw nigh to you"* (James 4:8). The one nearness is conditional upon the other. Man can never enjoy the sweetness of the Lord's presence unless the heart is reverently prepared to approach the mercy seat.

From the human side, this drawing nigh is beneficial. *"It is good for me to draw near to God"* (Psalm 73:28). Fellowship with Him is profitable for every part of life. A right attitude, however, is necessary for full communion. We must draw near with true hearts in the full assurance of faith. (See Hebrews 10:22.) *"Judas,"* we read, *"drew near unto Jesus to kiss him"* (Luke 22:47). May such a false approach never be ours!

From the divine side, the drawing near is sure yet silent. Quietly Jesus comes and places Himself alongside every circumstance and necessity of life. *"Thou drewest near in the day that I called upon thee: thou saidst, Fear not"* (Lamentations 3:57). It will be noticed that the Lord drew near to those disciples on the Emmaus road as they communed

---

36. Frances Brook, "My Goal Is God Himself."

about His blessed person. And this is ever so, for we can never experience His presence unless our conversation is fragrant with Himself. (See Malachi 3:16.)

There is, of course, a judicial nearness nothing can affect—

> Near, so very near to God,
> I cannot nearer be;
> For in the person of His Son
> I am as near as He.[37]

3. THE PARTNERSHIP ALL-CONDESCENDING—"WENT WITH THEM"

The crowning blessing of all is that the Lord goes with us over every road. He is the abiding Companion on the rugged highway. His name is Emmanuel—God with us. (See Matthew 1:23.) Our hearts are ravished as we think of the glories of Himself and of the joy of having Him closer to us than our own breath; but the marvel of His condescending grace is that He remains with us no matter where our lot is cast. *"I will never, never let go your hand"* (Hebrews 13:5 WEY). There are three sweet thoughts to observe just here.

He Journeyed with Them

It was a busy thoroughfare. Jostling crowds were on that road, but Jesus went with them all the way. And His partnership is not less real today. He is ever with us amid the duties of the home, the cares of business, and as we mingle with the crowds in the marketplace.

He Helped Them in Their Perplexities

Jesus made the hearts of those disciples glad through solving their hard problems. And as He continues to open the Scriptures, crooked places are made straight. Even if we do not understand all that we should, we know that He is with us and will ultimately make the mysterious plain.

---

37. William H. Havergal, "A Mind at Perfect Peace," 1847.

He Entered Their Homes

Not only was Jesus their Partner on the journey, walking and talking with them, but the One willing to share and enjoy the hospitality they offered Him. And those adoring hearts came to realize that Jesus was able to bless them, not only with His presence and person, but also with His provision.

His actual presence, however, was short-lived, for He vanished out of sight. Yet He is always with us. And it is the work of the Holy Spirit to make us conscious of His abiding nearness. May He go with us, then, into all our service and activities—out into all our cares, trials, sorrows, temptations, and joys! The consciousness of such a partnership will transfigure life at every point. The Lord is at hand! A devout soul was asked the secret of a life so beautiful and tranquil and unflurried, although constantly active. "You desire my secret? Here it is—I have a Friend!" Hast thou learned such a secret? Is Jesus your Friend, who blesses you with His nearness? Do you know Him as the Companion over the pilgrimage of life? If not, then ask Him this very moment to draw near and go with you as you journey on. And once He joins you, He will never leave you till traveling days are done.

ABOUT THE AUTHOR

When Dr. Herbert Lockyer (1886–1984) was first deciding on a career, he considered becoming an actor. Tall and well-spoken, he seemed a natural for the theater. But the Lord had something better in mind. Instead of the stage, God called Herbert to the pulpit, where, as a pastor, a Bible teacher, and the author of more than fifty books, he touched the hearts and lives of millions of people.

Dr. Lockyer held pastorates in Scotland and England for twenty-five years. As pastor of Leeds Road Baptist Church in Bradford, England, he became a leader in the Keswick Higher Life Movement, which emphasized the significance of living in the fullness of the Holy Spirit. This led to an invitation to speak at the Moody Bible Institute's fiftieth anniversary in 1936. His warm reception at that event led to his ministry in the United States. He received honorary degrees from both the Northwestern Evangelical Seminary and the International Academy of London.

In 1955, he returned to England, where he lived for many years. He then returned to the United States, where he spent the final years of his life in Colorado Springs, Colorado, with his son, the Rev. Herbert Lockyer Jr., a Presbyterian minister who eventually became his editor.

Welcome to Our House!

We Have a Special Gift for You ...

It is our privilege and pleasure to share in your love of Christian classics by publishing books that enrich your life and encourage your faith.

To show our appreciation, we invite you to sign up to receive a specially selected **Reader Appreciation Gift**, with our compliments. Just go to the Web address at the bottom of this page.

God bless you as you seek a deeper walk with Him!

WE HAVE A GIFT FOR YOU

whpub.me/classicthx

WHITAKER
HOUSE